GUILT TRIP
DETOX

GINA SANCHETTI AUSTIN

BALBOA.PRESS
A DIVISION OF HAY HOUSE

Balboa Press books may be ordered through booksellers or by contacting:

Balboa Press
A Division of Hay House
1663 Liberty Drive
Bloomington, IN 47403
www.balboapress.com
844-682-1282

Print information available on the last page.

ISBN: 978-1-9822-5064-5 (sc)
ISBN: 978-1-9822-5066-9 (hc)
ISBN: 978-1-9822-5065-2 (e)

Library of Congress Control Number: 2020912295

Balboa Press rev. date: 11/04/2020

CONTENTS

PREFACE

I AM OFTEN ASKED WHAT prompted me to write a book on guilt. People who know me find my choice of subject matter rather strange given my carefree nature. They assumed I never knew the word *guilt* existed. Little did they know that deep within me—actually, not that deep—I carried around a thick layer of guilt, that influenced many of my thoughts and decisions.

Feeling guilty can easily turn into a bad habit, and as with any bad habit, a conscious daily effort must be made to free yourself from its control in order to heal. Ridding oneself of years of manufactured guilt may take some time, but it is worth the effort in order to become empowered and live each day with more freedom, joy and peace of mind.

In the past, I wouldn't have dreamed of offering my point of view for fear of upsetting someone and subsequently dealing with the fallout of the "guilties."

However, I have grown from a person who cowered at expressing her thoughts to being a regular guest on two syndicated talk shows and voicing my opinion loudly and proudly. I was eventually dubbed the "relationship expert" because of my innate understanding of people's feelings and my ability to find solutions to their dating questions. By tuning out the manufactured rhetoric of the overbearing, finger-pointing "Guilt Monster," through the use of healthy boundaries, I have regained my peace of mind and am finally able to live a more fulfilling life.

Another reason I was prompted to write *Guilt Trip Detox* has much to do with my past profession. I was a flight attendant for over thirty years. On many flights, while I was conversing with crew and passengers alike, the *guilt* word made regular appearances. Many heartfelt stories included the phrase "I feel so guilty." When I asked each storyteller why he or she felt this way, the answer was generally "I don't know; I just do." There was always a fearful, doom-and-gloom uneasiness in people's demeanor when they mentioned the energy-sucking G-word.

Through countless conversations with folks from all walks of life, I noticed a common thread of "manufactured" guilt that occasionally dampened their otherwise sunny disposition. Out of sheer curiosity, I began to write down the seemingly endless types of guilt that people experienced. I then decided to investigate further to better understand what propels people to thrust guilt upon themselves needlessly and find solutions to release these debilitating thoughts.

Guilt Trip Detox covers fifty common types of guilt, found in a series of short stories, and offers advice to eradicate guilt from your system. I came to the conclusion that examining fifty types of some of the most recurring types of guilt would be a sufficient representation to enable readers to identify, understand, and rectify any additional self-imposed guilt they may experience along the way. As well, in order to make guilt tangible, I breathed life into a gigantic, lumbering, furry blue character called the Guilt Monster. The Guilt Monster's mandate is to make you believe you're always to blame for upsetting someone or yourself. This pleases the Guilt Monster to no end, because it has power over your thoughts, decisions, joy and ultimately controls your life. After reading *Guilt Trip Detox*, you will have learned how to identify the many facets of manufactured guilt and create boundaries to protect yourself from the debilitating effects of your nemesis, the Guilt Monster.

ACKNOWLEDGMENTS

I WOULD LIKE TO THANK the many people who supported me while I completed *Guilt Trip Detox*. Thank you to my parents, Ila and Arthur Sanchetti; my beautiful twin daughters, Angela and Alexandra; Aunt Laura; and many dear friends, colleagues, and family members who always kept the faith that this book would become a reality. Also, a special thank-you to Rob Duncan for aiding me throughout this journey with his expertise in the written word. You all fill my heart with joy.

INTRODUCTION

GUILT TRIP DETOX **WAS WRITTIN** to address those guilty thoughts that continue to seep into your being and offer solutions to banish them from your mind. You immerse yourself in guilt on and off throughout life. In your mind you feel as guilty as a hardened criminal because you've displeased someone or haven't lived up to others' standards, expectations, or beliefs. Perhaps you feel guilty because at some point in your life you made a grandiose error or showed extreme lack of judgment and feel you deserve to be endlessly punished, instead of forgiving and loving yourself, faults and all. Guilt may also stem from ingrained negative messaging received from your past, or perhaps it's the way your brain processes events in the light of low self-esteem or other variables. In the end, the *reasons* you feel guilty are not always flashing in neon lights in front of you, and fortunately their origins are not necessary in helping you heal. What will essentially aid you in extinguishing guilt forever is understanding the nature of the beast and knowing how to prevent it from manipulating your thoughts with its soul-sucking glare of shame and blame.

On the flip side, if you intentionally commit a cruel or malicious act and harm yourself or someone else, then, yes, you deserve to feel your soul temporarily squeezed by the Guilt Monster in order to awaken your conscience and make you think about your less than favorable actions. This type of guilt is not manufactured and is meant to enlighten you to your shortcomings. However, once you understand the lesson and strive to change for the better, even this type of guilt needs to be released if you are to live an emotionally happy and stable life. One purpose of being on this planet is to learn and grow from the many imperfect scenarios you will encounter. Soooo, cut yourself some slack and learn to cut loose the tether that tugs at your being that the Guilt Monster has placed upon you. Try to be a better person, make amends for your failures and oversights, and continue on your jouney through life unimpeded and guilt-free.

The Real Deal, or Manufactured?

Are you feeling the *real deal* type of guilt that is genuine and awakens your conscience to something you are doing wrong? Or are you experiencing the *manufactured* type because you feel guilty for no apparent reason. Either way, the full weight of the Guilt Monster is riding piggyback and jabbing its sharp, shiny spurs into your ribcage. When you feel guilty, this is usually a good time to dig deeper and ask yourself WHY! You may feel guilty because you don't feel worthy of having an opinion or doing something special for yourself. Maybe you did something intentionally that harmed someone. Whichever type of guilt you are experiencing, *real deal* or *manufactured*, it needs to be addressed and released.

Carrying around any type of guilt—whether it's self-loathing because you can't shed that extra weight or because you feel you have failed at something—will not only make you feel lousy, but will make you feel unworthy of reaching the heights of your destiny. Instead, nurture your feelings with tender reflection and compassion and then continue forward with your life. Do not allow yourself to continually become target practice for the Guilt Monster.

Keep track of each guilty thought in a journal, and then beside each thought, write what may have prompted you to feel that way. After reviewing whether the guilt was *real* and trying to enlighten you, or *manufactured* and toying with your mind, learn from it what you can and then dismiss it. This exercise will assist you in becoming conscious of what triggers your guilt, understanding it, and subsequently purging it from your system. With the guidance found in *Guilt Trip Detox*, you will discover methods to heal from the emotional drain of this habitual thought response.

Guilt Taskmaster

A *guilt taskmaster*, the Guilt Monster's best friend, is someone to be hyper aware of. Such an individual is astute at making others feel guilty to fulfill his or her agenda. Some *guilt taskmasters* utilize guilt out of sheer habit, and others are propelled by their craving for *control*; they may also possess a deep sense of insecurity, and getting their way at others' expense empowers them. It's a form of manipulation, and although it is not always executed consciously, it manages to have a debilitating effect on the recipient if not kept at bay.

Guilt taskmasters get their agendas filled by whimpering, batting their eyes, or using a sad, woe-is-me tone. Some *guilt taskmasters* were raised on a mountain of guilt themselves; therefore, it has become ingrained in them over the years and passed on out of sheer habit. Although the transference of guilt often cycles from generation to generation, worry not—*Guilt Trip Detox* will help you become aware of these energy-sucking tactics and empower you to deal with them head-on, enabling you to forever break free from the *guilt-chains* of the past. You will learn how to sever the hypnotic trance of the Guilt Monster through practicing mindfulness and setting boundaries.

If you've been under the spell of a *guilt taskmaster* (your mother or father, sibling, boss, coworker, friend, or your significant other) for a long period of time, you must become aware of identifying each guilt event that rears its ugly head. You will find this instructive as it will raise your awareness to the number of times the Guilt Monster has hijacked your thoughts, and therefore, your emotions. Through becoming increasingly *aware* of each guilty thought that seeps into the cracks of your mainframe, and protecting yourself with new boundaries, you will learn to reverse the debilitating spells cast upon you by the Guilt Monster.

When you get bowled over by the Guilt Monster's Mac truck of misery, and feel the full impact of blame and shame, it's time to read this book and heal. Brush off those nasty tread marks once and for all, because it's time to change the "guilties" into the "happies." Let's get started!

1 ABORTION GUILT

When you feel guilty about terminating an unplanned pregnancy

WOMEN (AS WELL AS MEN) may experience an overwhelming jolt of emotion after an abortion that can easily lead to **abortion guilt**. Their emotions slow-cook in a skillet of guilt for having created the scenario in the first place, then they turn up the heat until their feelings sizzle in flames of regret for having been so selfish. Additional layers of guilt thrust upon them by their parents, friends, religion, and society can leave them feeling browbeaten and worthless.

Having an abortion is a decision that affects everyone differently, and it is difficult to know beforehand how you may react after such a procedure. Some women say they feel little or no remorse after an abortion, and others feel a horrific, soul-wrenching guilt. One woman claimed that when she realized she was pregnant out of wedlock—and her boyfriend was unwilling to help raise their child, financially or otherwise—she was "damned if I do, and damned if I don't." She would feel damned if she *did* abort, as she would be encased in guilt for ending the life of her child, and damned if she *didn't* because she would have to raise her child alone in exceedingly difficult financial and emotional circumstances. In addition, her mom and siblings were not in a position to assist her, so this sweet pregnant woman felt abandoned in a wilderness of worry and shame. In the end, she carefully weighed her options and decided to have an abortion. This woman is now roommates with the Guilt Monster because she blames herself repeatedly for the less than perfect outcome. Unfortunately, life on Earth is far from perfect; therefore, her final judgment, whether right or wrong, should be looked upon as a coping and learning experience instead of constantly viewing it as a failure and living with a life sentence of remorse.

We all have some idea of what our limitations are, in particular when it comes to the demands of raising children. Any individual must assess if he or she has the mental, physical, and financial resources to bring a child into this world. It's a huge responsibility and one that should be taken seriously. If you feel the stirrings of guilt in the aftermath of an abortion, it is best to try to release the stored negative energy to regain peace of mind. Making executive decisions in life is never easy; therefore, realize you made your *best* decision at that particular moment and then move forward with what you have learned with a clear conscience.

When you are dealing with an unplanned pregnancy, take some time and do your homework to find the best solution for you. There are many organizations that offer information that will assist in your decision-making.

Consider all your options, and have faith that you will do what serves you best.

If you are perpetually suffering from the Guilt Monster shaking its rattle of shame at you after an abortion, there are several healing methods you can use to help dispel this image and ease the pain. Start by giving your aborted child a name. Send the child your love, and ask him or her for forgiveness. You may also write the child's name on a piece of paper, set the paper near a lit candle, and talk about why you opted to abort and how you feel about your decision in the present moment. Say everything you need to say, and unload every emotion buried within. This may take days, months or longer, but it will assist in purging the guilt associated with your decision. Next, when you feel you have said all you need to say, burn the paper in a ceremonial fire, or place it in a box and bury it in order to give the matter a sense of closure.

Forgive yourself, and if you are spiritual, ask God to forgive you. You may also find it beneficial to ask your unborn child to forgive you as well. Just don't allow the experience to forever darken your days with shame. If guilt persists, join a group where you can discuss your feelings with others, or if you prefer a more private setting, talk to a professional one-on-one, either at his or her office or on the phone. If you're unsure where to begin, ask your doctor or do a Google search to find the ideal forum for you.

Please refrain from endlessly judging and condemning yourself for choices made under duress in an imperfect world; it is unnecessary to continually persecute yourself. It is debilitating, and in the end will not serve you well.

You did what you thought was necessary at that moment in time, case closed! Give yourself credit for having the courage to follow through on such an enormous decision. Learn from the experience, and continue your journey with love in your heart instead of living under a dome of regret and sadness. The image of the Guilt Monster gleefully pushing your empty stroller of shame must be banished forever from your thoughts. You deserve joy and peace in your life, but only you can create it and allow yourself deliverance.

2 ACCOMMODATION GUILT

When you feel guilty about not finding enough time for everyone

ARE YOU FEELING GUILTY ABOUT *not* being available for everyone, *not* answering all your emails or cell phone each time it rings, or *not* being able to attend each and every function? The truth of the matter is that there are only so many minutes in a day, and sometimes you are simply unable to accommodate everyone. You then begin to feel the bubbling of **accommodation guilt** because you put others' expectations in a big ol' caldron on the back burner, leaving the Guilt Monster in charge of stirring it up oh so unlovingly. I am not suggesting you become ridiculously selfish and cease giving a you-know-what about any you-know-whos. I am simply trying to make you realize that it's impossible to be available 24/7 to satisfy the many expectations of the world, and there is no need to feel guilty about it. It is important to take care of yourself first and foremost, and when time is short, others will simply have to wait. Therefore, learn to prioritize what's most important to you, and if need be, solidify it by writing it down as a reminder. This way you are less inclined to be swayed by the endless desires of others.

As you get older, life seems to get busier and more hectic. Caring for your loved ones while attending to a plethora of daily responsibilities requires a lot of time and energy. Whether buying groceries, visiting your mom, going to the dentist, doctor, or helping with homework, your days can fill up at the speed of light. If you are unable to wish everyone a happy birthday on Facebook, attend Uncle Bart's birthday party, or play yet another golf game, there is absolutely no need to feel **accommodation guilt**. Besides, the Guilt Monster is a lousy caddy.

Instead of allowing the seven-hundred-pound Guilt Monster to perform *Riverdance* on your neurotransmitters, simply communicate to others that you are unable to attend. It is not necessary to divulge the reasons *why* you are unavailable; however, if asked, do so at your discretion. If someone gives you grief and makes you feel guilty for not being available, just remain firm or as a last resort, cut the conversation short. How others react to your decision is not your concern. No one understands your time constraints better than you, so don't allow the Guilt Monster the power to make you feel uncomfortable as it squeezes you with its suffocating hug of shame.

I recall feeling **accommodation guilt** when my teenage daughter broke her arm and I was out of town. With all the motherly instincts I could muster, I spoke to her for over an hour on the phone to help her through this difficult time. After I hung up, and although I knew I was going to be home soon, I was paralyzed with guilt for not being able to be by her side. *I should have been there!* and *What kind of a mother am I?* kept echoing in my head. My darling daughter did not deserve this abandonment at such a critical time. I felt the Guilt Monster was going to take her to Child and Family Services because I was an unfit mom. Obviously, it was ridiculous to feel this way given the circumstances of being physically unable to be by her side, but guilt and logic—much like oil and water—don't mix well. In hindsight, I should not have felt guilty at all. I was simply away at work at the time of the accident, but when I heard the distress in my daughter's voice, my emotions hijacked my rational thought, and I felt inundated with guilt.

As soon as I got home, I gave my daughter a big hug and told her how sorry I was that she had had to deal with her experience alone. Acknowledging her emotions made her feel loved and cared for. My apology was unnecessary, but appreciated. My daughter was happy I was home and fully understood there was nothing I could have changed in order to be with her when she broke her arm. She knew I'd done my best by calling her, and she'd felt great comfort from hearing my voice and knowing I would soon be by her side. I later realized I had felt immense guilt for no reason. I manufactured it because I blamed myself for not being home to comfort my daughter; however, I had no way of knowing it was going to happen. Therefore, that train of thought made no sense, nor did my guilt. Instead of praising myself for being a responsible parent and doing the best I could with the tools I was given, I allowed guilt to hijack my rational thought, tamper with my emotions, and put them in a tailspin. After reviewing the situation further, I realized my **accommodation guilt** was totally self-inflicted. I then dragged the Guilt Monster by its mangy blue coat, kicking and screaming, along with my worn-out Supermom cape, and hurled them both into the nearest dumpster never to be seen again. Buh-bye!

3 ADDICTION GUILT

*When you feel guilty about your
failures in combatting addiction*

WE LIVE IN A WORLD plagued by addictions—everything
from food, drugs, alcohol, and sex to all sorts of
unconventional things, such as eating soil or toilet paper.
The list of addictions is long and would easily fill another
book. Having said that, I find there is one thing that
addicts have in common: They feel **addiction guilt** about
their uncontrollable urges as they sense the judgmental
eyes of everyone upon them, including their own.

Addiction is a complex disease of the brain. When
you become addicted, you develop strong impulses that
you have difficulty controlling. Simply having someone
repeatedly tell you to stop your destructive behavior will
most likely not work. Although there is no silver bullet
for addiction, there are a host of treatments available
depending on the nature and severity of the dependency.

When you have attempted to overcome your addiction
and fall short of victory, you blame yourself for not attaining
your goal, and quickly become the recipient of the Guilt

Monster's sledgehammer falling squarely upon you. Once again you have let down your family, friends, and most importantly yourself and have failed to meet everyone's high expectations. You feel like a failure for being so weak and undisciplined. You want to hide far away from the world, and consequently, you collapse deeper into the comforting arms of what put you there in the first place: your addiction.

Addictions take a great deal of courage, willpower, and—most often—outside assistance to overcome. When you feel beaten down because you continue to fall off the wagon of recovery, you must try your best not to add another debilitating layer of negativity to the mix, such as guilt. This will only act as a road block and weaken your resolve, sap your willpower, and impede your recovery.

A struggling alcoholic claimed to have been sober for three years. Two months later, however, after a drunken episode, she was forcibly taken away by two constables and charged with public intoxication and refusing arrest. Because this was a serious setback, she felt the immediate onset of defeat and the sting of humiliation envelop her soul. In her eyes, she saw herself as a failure deserving of nothing more than punishment. But self-punishment is never the answer. It is normal to experience failure when in recovery, so be gentle with yourself when it occurs. There was no need for this lady to equate failure with guilt and immerse herself in shame, blame and misery, which resulted in her consumption of more alcohol to numb her troubled soul. This is the *last* thing this addict should subject herself to after a setback. It compounds the problem and creates an atmosphere that can push any person off the precipice of hope and into a downward spiral of dejection. Strength, courage, compassion, hope and forgiveness are some of the tools needed to combat addiction, not guilt! It's a matter of choice how you decide to feel, whether it's a day of guilt or a day of hope. Always choose the latter as it will assist you immensely in achieving the results you seek.

Some treatments for addiction are: detoxification for drugs and alcohol (usually done under medical supervision), short-or long-term residential treatment, psychotherapy, family therapy, group therapy, twelve-step programs, medication, meditation, and exercise. Also, it is recommended that you have a few good friends on standby in case of emergency, or when you require immediate support during your most vulnerable times.

When guilt starts seeping into the cracks of your brokenness because you feel you have failed to beat your addiction, plug the gap with positive, gentle, loving thoughts to release yourself from the lonely confines of manufactured guilt. The Guilt Monster recoils at such behavior, and will eventually wither and die as it realizes it no longer has anything negative to feed off to sustain itself.

Create strong boundaries to protect yourself from the temptations of addiction. Find new friends if your old ones sabotage your efforts, sometimes unwittingly, and lure you back into the abyss. Spend time with like-minded people who protect you, want you to heal, and support every step of your recovery.

Continue your rehabilitation program without the Guilt Monster barging in and waving a scorecard in your face, endlessly judging you and making you feel like less of a person when you have a weak moment or thought. You have the power within you to succeed, and **addiction guilt** only casts a menacing shadow on your strength and conviction. *Be* resilient and brave, *be* proactive, and *be*lieve in yourself, and it will *be* a *be*autiful tomorrow. Your spirit is your inner strength and God given gift, and must be protected from negativity at all times. Instead of falling off the wagon of recovery and feeling guilty, push the Guilt Monster off your wagon, and keep on rolling peacefully into the sunset with only your determined spirit riding shotgun.

4 ANGER GUILT

When you feel guilty about losing your composure

ALTHOUGH YOU CONSIDER YOURSELF A decent person and try your best to get along with everyone, there are occasions when someone pushes your neon red anger button, catapulting your emotional restraint into another hemisphere. Before anger is unleashed, you feel the bubbling lava of irritability in your veins and simultaneously a mounting pressure preparing to release. You try to remain calm and suppress your temper, but it's a losing battle. Then *kapow!* You say things to someone you don't mean to say, you do things you thought you could never do, and you feel an inner rage you are unable to control.

When your anger "pilot light" has been lit and someone throws a gallon of fuel on it, you have the potential to retaliate with words and actions you will not be proud of. Stomping, throwing things, and slamming doors are just a few of the ways you may express your raw emotions. And if you are really rolling in the mud, you may even strike someone or worse. That is why it is best to remove yourself from emotionally charged situations as they have a way of escalating at the speed of light. If drugs and alcohol are involved, it exponentially increases the possibility of an angry outburst. When you have been involved in a situation where you lost your composure and the dust of your anger begins to settle, there's a good chance you will be the recipient of the Guilt Monster riding its steamroller of shame and regret over you, crushing you with **anger guilt**.

You begin to reflect upon your postvolcanic behavior and imperfect humanness, wishing you could take back the hurtful words that bypassed the restraints of your civility—words that inflicted pain and heartbreak on the receiver, words that weren't necessarily true, but at the time you were feeling sorry for yourself, wearing the victim hat and lashing out. Words are powerful, and unfortunately in this circumstance, have the ability to leave a damaging imprint on the receiver that can reverberate in their minds for many days to come.

Knowing how poorly you reacted, you want to penalize yourself. You instinctively punish yourself by feeling **anger guilt**. Although you reacted in a less than desirable fashion, keep in mind that you are human, and getting angry is a normal part of your emotional makeup. Although it is best to avoid heated situations, look at them as a learning experience that allows you to become better acquainted with your emotional trigger points.

Once the dust settles post argument, and you realize your emotions took over the flight controls of your composure, it's best to clear the air with the person on the receiving end of your anger, if possible, through calm and honest communication. Apologize to the person in question, and let them know what triggered your anger in the first place. If the other person is not interested in your heartfelt explanation and apology and wants nothing more to do with you, chalk it up to experience and continue living guilt-free with the new and improved YOU. You've done all you can to rectify the situation; therefore, if the other person involved cannot find forgiveness in his or her heart, that is THEIR lesson to learn and therefore there is nothing to feel guilty about. Unfortunately, not everyone is capable of instantly forgiving another without hesitation, if ever, so do not let someone else's character flaws, soul development, or overall processing of the situation perpetuate your burden of guilt.

In future, if you feel provoked and are entering the *anger zone*, it's best to remain silent and/or walk away from ground zero before you say or do things you wish you hadn't. Perhaps take an emotional time-out by distancing yourself until you calm down and process the situation. Allow some much-needed time for the boiling emotions of all concerned to simmer before revisiting the situation to do damage control; given time, cooler heads will see things more rationally and will prevail.

The Guilt Monster will try to stoke your **anger guilt**, hoping you will continually berate yourself and feel awful about your less than favorable actions forever. This is its goal because the monster feeds off guilt. Do not allow this twisted mind-set to control and negatively affect you! After an anger episode, all that is required is a review of the scenario in order to learn something from it, offer an apology if necessary, and forgive yourself and others. Forgiveness is essential, as we are all perpetually learning about our imperfections.

The more you figure out how to avoid anger traps through calm communication, the more you will learn to deal with provocation or sensitive issues minus emotional drama. In the meantime, be on high alert of anger's turbulant jet stream. Through the growing awareness of your triggers and your improved communication skills, you will become a master of your emotions. Wipe clean the menacing stains of **anger guilt** that the Guilt Monster has left lingering in your conscience, and start each day with understanding in your heart and a chance to start anew.

5 BAD MOOD GUILT

*When you feel guilty about how
your bad mood reflects on others*

WE ALL HAVE A WIDE range of emotions, and I believe it is healthy to express all of them when necessary. However, when you find you are frequently sad or in a bad mood, you may consider yourself a burden on those around you and experience **bad mood guilt.** Although at times you try to hide your moodiness, because you don't want to bring anyone down, others easily see through it. When your bad mood has been revealed, you instantaneously feel guilty for contaminating the joy of those around you, and feel like a failure.

A bad mood often acts as a catalyst to unlock parts of your life that require your attention. It brings to the forefront matters that you may have buried or weren't aware of until something triggered their existence. When uncomfortable feelings are rumbling deep within you, they have the ability to shoot to the surface unannounced in the form of a bad mood.

Look at your bad mood positively, as it offers an opportunity to take some time to meditate on what got you feeling so lousy in the first place. Focusing on your wants, needs, and desires will help shed some light on the root of your bad mood so you become enlightened to possible adjustments in your life that will better serve you. It's all part of your growth and evolution, so do not always look upon a bad mood as a negative.

Bad mood guilt arises when you judge yourself for being less than perfect because you aren't jovial all of the time. However, nobody is in a perfect mood all the time; therefore, why judge? Actually, bad moods should be allowed to surface instead of being left to fester, as they are an indicator of something troubling you. It is actually thereaputic to talk to others about your bad mood. Not only will they lend an ear to your frustrations, but they also act as a sounding board. Those who are concerned about you will want to help because they care, so make it easier on them by divulging some of your inner frustration instead of them going on a psychological archaeological dig. Sharing your feelings with those you can trust is a fail-safe way to feel better quickly. It unbridles your emotional angst and allows someone with a different point of view an opportunity to help solve your problem. Also, by sharing your plight with others, it has a double positive effect. Not only are the recipients of your bad mood helping YOU feel better, THEY feel elevated by doing a good deed. As well, they will be more inclined to come forward when they need THEIR spirits lifted.

If you feel you are being judged by someone while in

the midst of your bad mood, communicate to that person that you are not having a great day. If the person continues to be disturbed by your moodiness, maybe he or she lacks compassion, or perhaps is not comfortable dealing with intense emotions. Whatever the reason, do not take it personally, which will only fuel your guilt. There is no need to have the Guilt Monster pound you deeper into the pavement than you already are.

Also, I know people who never let on that they are in a bad mood because they feel it displays weakness. They give the impression that they can handle anything, anytime, anywhere! But this does not demonstrate how they *really* feel and also paints a false picture to others that their life is beyond perfect. When others are in a bad mood or having a bad day, they may feel like failures in the eyes of the "perfect ones", but the truth of the matter is that *everyone* experiences bad moods; some just express it more than others. It would be a tragically lonely world if no one ever divulged their feelings to others and felt forever entrapped in their tormented thoughts.

It is becoming common knowledge that storing negative feelings is not conducive to the maintenance of good health. Repressed, unacknowledged emotions block the natural flow of your positive energy. Divulging your feelings to a confidant will set your soul free and help you gain better perspective. No one can read your mind or feelings unless you *share* them, so dump the **bad mood guilt** and set yourself free by expressing yourself instead. I guarantee you'll feel relieved once you release your innermost thoughts from your mind's firmly sealed pressure cooker.

Take comfort in knowing you are not alone in how you feel. It's healthy and normal to share emotional burdens with friends and family members, instead of *guilt-shaming* yourself. Heck, sometimes it's great to unload your troubles on your hairdresser or a total stranger. People with whom you are not closely associated with tend to be more upfront when offering advice, because they are not directly affected by your emotional fallout. They feel free to deliver their unbridled opinion without copious layers of sugarcoating that a family member may dole out. Sometimes, clear and concise advice is just what you need to get to the bottom of your bad mood instead of more *hand-holding* conversations that avoid the obvious for fear of hurting your feelings.

There are many reasons why we have *bad days* and you are entitled to your share. Life is sometimes a minefield of compressed learning curves that have a way of temporarily collapsing your lighthearted spirit. Always remain patient and hopeful when dealing with emotional dips on your mainframe. I understand that too many curveballs can leave you feeling overwhelmed, depleted, and moody; however, I assure you, your bad mood phase is normal and will pass eventually.

If, however, your bad mood becomes a daily routine, you may want to determine why you repeatedly react this way. It could be a bad habit that keeps recurring and needs to be eradicated through positive mindfulness, or it may be a deeper, more complex problem that arose from childhood or a past event. Talk to your doctor if your bad mood persists as you may require medication, counselling, a vacation, or all three. As a rule, bad moods are temporary, but please do not wait to see a doctor if yours continues long term and is causing constant, inexplicable sadness and dark thoughts.

Throughout life, it is helpful to march forth with daily positive affirmations to assist you in training your emotions to become more positive. Dwelling too long on negative aspects will only obliterate the focus of the positive moments that continue to surround you. A statement such as "I accept peace, joy, and harmony in my life" is an example of filling your mind with positive affirmations. I'm not suggesting that you whitewash your feelings at the risk of discounting relevant issues that need to be addressed. I am simply saying you should try to remain positive, through the use of affirmations, while simultaneously finding the root of your bad mood. You may also find it helpful to go to your bookstore for information regarding additional methods to get in touch with your feelings, such as *Feelings Buried Alive Never Die* by Karol K. Truman. When you work on expressing yourself and you press on, it will "de-press" the Guilt Monster, and your **bad mood guilt** will be gone.

6 BREAKUP GUILT

*When you feel guilty about
ending a relationship*

WHEN YOU FEEL UNHAPPY AND stuck in a relationship, and the joy of being together is on a permanent vacation, you may be headed for a *breakup*. The person you are breaking up with may be wonderful; however, your emotions and lives are headed in opposite directions. You feel the full force of **breakup guilt** because making a change to your status will undoubtedly hurt and disappoint others. The Guilt Monster is seen loitering on the top balcony of your heart, wagging its finger at you in disgust. Although blame and guilt are fast becoming your best friends, you feel you have only one choice to regain peace of mind, and that is to find the courage to end a lifeless relationship and move forward.

Unfortunately, there is the possibility of feeling a tremendous amount of guilt associated with a relationship breakup, whether it is personal or work related. A breakup has the ability to affect one's feelings on many levels. The longer the union, the more emotionally complex a breakup can be because of the history shared. Your history includes relationships with other family members or employees, joint finances, shared belongings and properties, as well as copious memories. Although you have given extensive thought to terminating the relationship and feel relieved about your decision, your parade of freedom continues to be rained on by massive guilt drops from the Guilt Monster's black cloud of blame.

If dissolving a relationship becomes a necessity for your mental and physical health, then it is the correct decision. Post-breakup, continue to retain a certain amount of compassion for those on the receiving end of your decision, even if it means dodging airborne china along the way. Whatever the reactionary fallout may be, try to remain considerate and calm, and if necessary, run for the hills until the dust settles.

Because relationships are in close proximity to our hearts, it often takes time to process emotions when a breakup occurs. We are all emotional beings with a propensity to react differently to change. During these transitional times, be mindful that feelings are fragile and usually go through an intricate rerouting, including shock, denial, anger, loneliness, and sadness, in order to process the magnitude of the situation. This is why it is important to allow someone the necessary time to digest the *breakup* news. These emotions are natural, and not a reason to feel guilty. One way of absolving **breakup guilt** is to view your decision as a way of doing a favor for the other person or "breakee." You found the courage to take a leap of faith and move on from an unmanageable situation, allowing your former partner the freedom to find a more satisfying fit elsewhere.

I understand that all relationships, whether work or love related, get stagnant at times. However, when you are devoid of emotion, repeatedly disrespected, or have become utterly miserable and numb and have exhausted all possible solutions, it's time to change course. Although that part of your life has come to an end, make sure the Guilt Monster isn't waiting around the corner to be your sequel. As long as you are being civil and fair during a *breakup*, there is no need to allow the Guilt Monster to hang your dirty laundry out to dry on its clothesline of blame along with your freshly signed divorce decree or resignation papers.

7 CAREGIVING GUILT

When you feel guilty about not providing sufficient care for a loved one

CAREGIVING HAS THE FULL-BLOWN POTENTIAL to turn into a full-time job. When you are responsible for someone's care, there are numerous tasks that need to be addressed, from endless appointments to the person's most basic necessities. Most of us, at some point in our lives, will have to care for an aging parent, partner, or friend. As they age and become more vulnerable, they will require additional assistance. These obligations can easily snowball and carve into your personal time and responsibilities.

When I worked full time as a flight attendant, I was out of town half the week. I maintained my house and children's lives, and twice a month I cared for my autistic brother. That alone is a heavy load, and then there was my aging parents' needs. Needless to say, my responsibility plate was overflowing. Instead of taking an occassional time-out to replenish myself with a soothing bubble bath drizzled with essential oils, the Guilt Monster would dump an ice-cold pail of guilt over my head as I contemplated whether

I should be tending to more caregiving responsibilities instead.

Finding some quiet time to decompress and rejuvenate my mind and body in the soothing hot water of my bath has always been my way of recharging my batteries and should never be looked upon as a *guilty pleasure*. **Caregiving guilt** easily has the potential to lead to burnout unless you create firm boundaries and etch some much-deserved personal time into your itinerary for relaxation and fun.

In order to achieve balance in your life, it is essential to create and adhere to your boundaries. I am not saying you should abandon your caregiving responsibilities; however, in order to replenish your weary soul, communicate your needs to those you care for so they are aware. Also consider delegating duties to other family members or outside services to help lessen your workload and keep your spirits elevated.

A woman with advanced Alzheimer's who lives in a care facility, also lives in a different city from her four children. Although she does not recognize them anymore, they still visit her a few times a year. Their mom used to love reading books, but now that she is unable, her children decided to hire someone to come in a few hours a week to read to her. It was a favorable solution that allowed her children to continue living their lives without constantly worrying about their mom's welfare. Knowing their mom had all her necessities being met as well as the added comfort of being read to, gave the children peace of mind and quashed any guilt. If, however, you cannot afford to pay for outside services or a care facility, you may seek out other helpful agencies subsidized by your local government. Your physician may also be able to direct you to additional available resources. Whatever the case, do not allow **caregiving guilt** to take over your thoughts when someone's basic needs are being properly met. You are providing the person in question with the essentials, and in some cases, more; therefore, drop the guilt!

Be mindful that your caregiving routine does not become so overwhelming that you slide into depression or have a meltdown. Review your boundaries often, and make it a point to pencil in some necessary fun time every week so you have something to look forward to. Spending quality time with friends, taking in a movie or concert, going on a leisurely walk, or reading a book are all examples of doing things that will keep your spirit nourished. Even going out to have a quick cup of coffee has the power to take the focus off your responsibility overload and allow you a reprieve. Always make time to vent, laugh, and relax; a few precious moments of levity aids immensely in keeping your spirit well-oiled.

If you have a child who has special needs, or you've recently given birth, it is wise to seek outside help to occasionally allow yourself a much-needed break. This can be in the form of a family member, home care, specialized schooling, or playtime with a sitter or professional care provider. Do not douse yourself in **caregiving guilt** thinking you are "abandoning" your son or daughter. You are not! You are allowing your child to be cared for by someone trustworthy other than yourself, that is all. After your respite, you will feel refreshed and be in a better position to give your best to those you love, instead of becoming drained, miserable, and depressed.

As of late I broke my ankle and had to rely on others for my most basic needs. I didn't want anyone to feel overwhelmed or guilty for not helping me enough, so I delegated tasks to others based on their itinerary, expertise, and comfort level. Everyone was able to participate in my convalescing without getting burned out. Everyone got a chance to cook, buy groceries, do laundry or whatever task they chose. They felt connected to my healing without feeling guilty. The key to caregiving is to keep YOUR life in balance with those you care for. It's not always an easy task to create balance, but well worth the effort to keep your engine running on all cylinders. Your body and mind will thank you.

Caregiving is not for the faint of heart and requires a great deal of organization, time, patience, strength, and compassion. It's a tall order and a perpetual balancing act as you tend not only to your needs but also to the daily needs of another. If you become overwhelmed, take a time out and re-etch your boundaries. As well, there are many groups you can join in order to exchange ideas and discover alternative coping solutions. Always remember to take care of your mental and physical health first or else you will become exhausted and unavailable to care for the needs of another. In order for your voyage to remain happily afloat, throw the excessive demands of the Guilt Monster off your caregiving boat.

8 CHEATING/LUST GUILT

When you feel guilty about betraying your significant other

YOU'RE AT A PARTY WITH your significant other. Leaning against the wall, on the opposite side of the room, is a well-dressed charismatic person. Your eyes lock, your heart starts to beat faster, your brain gets foggy, and you have temporarily forgotten the person with whom you came to this soiree. Oh no … you suddenly find yourself lusting for another person! This has never happened to you while in your present relationship. What is going on? Your emotions begin to spin out of control. Simultaneously you feel **lust guilt** for having sexual thoughts about another. Your significant other notices your mind is a million miles away and asks what you're so deep in thought about. Do you tell the truth and start a jealous quarrel, or do you take the path of avoidance and lie? You decide on the latter, along with the accompanying backlash of guilty indigestion, as the Guilt Monster offers you a tainted hors d'oeuvre.

In some cases, there may be more to your lustful gaze and palpitating heartbeat than just a passing fancy. You ask yourself why you've become so entranced with a complete stranger who has the power to make your heart go pitter-patter, something you have not felt in your present relationship in a very long time. Perhaps the chemistry with another awoke a part of you that feels unacknowledged or unloved in your current relationship.

Whatever the reason, give yourself the necessary time to focus on and process your feelings. If you are constantly wondering what it would be like to be in a relationship with another, then it may be time to discuss your issues with your partner instead of sweeping them under that big ol' Egyptian rug of yours. Sometimes lustful thoughts act as a catalyst to awaken unresolved feelings you've buried deep within yourself. Are you sexually curious about being with another person, or are you simply bored with your current partner or situation? Perhaps you hold animosity toward your partner for something he or she did in the past, and cheating, whether it takes place in your mind or physically, is a form of retribution. Whatever the reasons, I recommend giving your lustful thoughts some deep consideration.

Having a good heart-to-heart with your significant other is an excellent way to get to the bottom of why you have amorous thoughts about another. In my estimation, intimacy with another is more cerebral than physical, so communication is key to resolving relationship issues before things escalate and there's no turning back. If, however, you are in a situation where your lust is going to *bust* your relationship because it has ventured into the red zone of disloyalty, the Guilt Monster, with its two left feet, may become your new tango partner.

If your lust has evolved into a sexual encounter, it is only fair to tell your significant other about your moment of weakness and express your regret in order to salvage the relationship and extinguish **cheating guilt**. Although you did not intend to hurt your partner while your brain got stuck in your libido, which was in overdrive by the way, the Guilt Monster has a right to pounce on you for crossing the loyalty line. This will help you realize you were out of line, and make you aware of not repeating the offense in the future. If you manage to dodge the Guilt Monster's bullet after your betrayal, and can live without divulging your affair to your partner, I urge you to learn from this oversight and never, ever repeat the offense again, as infidelity is not conducive to a healthy, long-lasting relationship. Eventually, habitual patterns of betrayal will bite you in the you-know-what!

If, after you expose the infidelity, your significant other is unable to forgive you, please do not continue to blame yourself and tolerate the endless lashings of **cheating guilt**. It happened, you cleared your conscience, and it now remains in the past. Although you had to pay for absolution with dire consequences, you and your clear conscience may now move into the future, stronger and wiser. The lesson has been learned, so there is no need to revisit the Guilt Monster's party of shame.

It is normal to feel the lingering sting of a hard-learned lesson, so be patient and gentle with yourself while you regroup. Eventually the swelling from your guilt sting will subside. You will grow from the situation, create new boundaries, and forgive yourself. You are human, and it is NORMAL to sometimes go off course in life's ocean of possibilities. Each day acts as a test to discover how you tick, what you desire, and what you can and cannot live with in your heart of hearts.

Some life lessons can temporarily take the wind out of your sails, so allow yourself some time to digest the situation, learn from it, make amends, and sail on with the added wisdom gained. As long as you are not a repeat offender and unconscionably hurting others, the Guilt Monster should not be doing its happy dance while nailing a shingle on your door that reads "Cheater Lives Here."

9 CHILD-REARING GUILT

*When you feel guilty about not
providing enough for your children*

AS A PARENT, YOU TRY to provide your child the best that life has to offer, sometimes to the extent of becoming financially, physically, or emotionally overwhelmed. How did you start believing that giving more to your child is necessarily better? Some kids are not even remotely interested in all the gifts and opportunities their parents try so desperately to provide. Giving it *all* to your kids has become an obsession, perhaps because previous generations did not have access to an abundance of *things*. You feel that if you do not supply your children with all the riches and opportunities you can squeeze out of your hectic life and strained bank account, you are a leper in the parenting world. Not true!

Do you have a guilt cloud hanging over you if little Johnny down the street is involved in more sports, has better equipment, and works with an amazing math tutor—things your children don't have because of financial reasons or time constraints? You may also experience

child-rearing guilt when you come home exhausted and stressed from work and have little energy left to play with your children or help them with homework. In order to block out your manufactured guilt and get back in their good graces, you utilize the almighty dollar and try to *buy* their love and attention. This is a perfect scenario for the Guilt Monster to play *Let's Make a Deal*. Jennifer gets a new cell phone and Thomas gets a new drum kit. The guilt trip is well on its way with no end in sight.

Stop berating yourself for being unable to squeeze more extracurricular activities into your children's day and feeling like a parental failure if your kids are at home puttering around with you in the backyard. Time spent at home is also important in your children's development. It makes them feel safe and loved, and grants them several opportunities to bond with you, as well as learn basic life skills; all of which develop confidence. Sometimes a lot of doing and talking isn't necessary; just watching a movie together will give your kids a sense of security and make them feel safe from all the stuff whirling around them in this fast-paced world. With both parents working, and family time at a premium, I feel it is more important than ever to spend quality time with your children in the midst of life's daily hustle.

If you repeatedly spoil your children because you are trying to compensate for your supposed less than perfect parenting skills or lack of time, you will be steering them in the direction of *entitlement*, which, once attained, is a tough habit to break. Also, fulfilling every desire on your children's wishlist may easily run the risk of diluting their drive and creativity. Personal drive is created by a deep desire to attain something. In order to fulfill that desire, one must become creative to figure out how to accomplish the goal. If a parent is constantly coming to the rescue and providing their kids' every want, need, and desire, it becomes learned behavior for the children to simply sit idle and await parental direction. They know that if they hold back long enough, Mom and Dad will deal with their problems, buy them what they want, and serve it to them on a silver platter. This is not positive messaging as it will not teach your children how to develop drive, cope with disappointment, deal with imperfection, and problem-solve.

Some of the people with the most groundbreaking and evolutionary ideas had poor to average upbringings. So how did they succeed? They had to be creative in order to get what they wanted because there were no handouts. Have faith, dear parents; your children will find their way in this big, beautiful world without your breaking the bank to put them in yet another extracurricular activity or buying their love with another unwarranted gift.

Start detoxing from **child-rearing guilt** today and reclaim your power! Pat yourself on the back for being an awesome parent, instead of being berated by the Guilt Monster wielding your kid's idle baseball bat. As well, there is no need to feel guilty about altering the house rules as you become aware of *guiltless* ways to raise your children. Explain to them why you are making alterations to the status quo, so they understand where you're coming from, and don't think you blew a gasket somewhere along the way.

Love and acknowledgment are key to a happy home, and your children will feel empowered when they are "in the loop" regarding your feelings and the house rules instead of receiving the Band-Aid of another meaningless *guilt gift*. Also, do NOT give yourself the third degree because you did not figure out better parenting skills sooner. There is no user manual attached to your baby when they are born, sooo… know in your heart that you are doing your best to raise your child without the Guilt Monster dragging your weary body through endless malls or team practices to appease your guilt. Your acknowledgement, caring words, and love will take your kids further than will any new car in the driveway on their sixteenth birthday, bought and paid for by the Guilt Monster.

10 CHORES GALORE GUILT

When you feel guilty about not completing your to-do list

DAY IN AND DAY OUT you scamper around your house like a panting Pomeranian, tending to chores and feeling guilty if you don't get 'er all done. Somewhere in that brain of yours you've decided that you will feel guilty if you don't complete every chore on your list in record time. As it turns out, no one actually cares about your efforts but you. In addition, you are setting yourself up for failure and disappointment before you get started, because the Guilt Monster's scroll of things to do is endless. You become stressed and overwhelmed as you decide to work faster and harder, but more chores seem to arise out of nowhere. Once you cross something off the to-do list, it is usually replaced with two or three additional chores. Instead of taking two steps forward and one step back, you feel yourself slipping into a giant pail filled with cleaning agents. This mindset of feeling swamped with chores creates anxiety and can easily overwhelm you as you feverishly work faster to get the jobs done! However, if you don't jump off the treadmill of chores to take an occasional breather, you will eventually run out of steam, slow down, and do a face-plant. Having fun yet?

It's wonderful to be proactive about your chores, but there's a limit to how much you can accomplish. Don't get a bad case of **chores galore guilt** because you haven't reached the illusory finish line. As it turns out, completing your chores is not an Olympic sport, nor is there a grand prize or trophy for the winner with your name engraved on it, so relax. If you don't check off all the boxes of your to-do list, don't automatically think you are selfish, lazy, or a failure and feel guilty about it. This false internal messaging of inadequacy must stop because it is harmful to your self-esteem and overall joy. Instead of fretting over your constantly growing chore list, give yourself a standing ovation for the chores you HAVE managed to complete.

While tending to your chores, it's good practice to slot a "you moment" and take a well-deserved break. Taking breaks from the monotony of chores allows you to refuel and, in the end, makes you happier and more productive. Have lunch with a friend, watch some television, or enjoy the bliss of a little retail therapy as a reward for your hard work. Everything and everyone will have to come to a grinding halt while you find time to just *be*. It's called *respecting* yourself. When you respect yourself and adhere to healthy boundaries, you are happier and others tend to respect you as well. Keep your boundaries at the ready to maintain "chore balance" and avoid the Guilt Monster's large paws pushing you toward yet another task. Always remember to find time to *pamper as you scamper*.

Write your to-do list for the day and review it to see if it seems reasonable. If not, throw some chores out the door until another day. You have nothing to lose except the irritating demands of the Guilt Monster, who's hurling yet another bottle of Windex at you from across the room. With your new boundaries firmly in place, soon your **chores galore guilt** will be a thing of the past. Now that you've become reasonable about the amount of time needed to complete your tasks, and have become a master at creating some downtime, put your feet up and turn on Netflix. With the Guilt Monster no longer barking orders at you and cracking the whip in your frontal lobe, your bitterness, exhaustion, and anxiety will soon be seen parasailing off your mountain of chores, never to be seen again.

11 CULTURAL GUILT

When you feel guilty for not living up to cultural expectations

I HAVE TALKED TO PEOPLE of many ethnicities and cultures and have heard a common theme in their stories: Guilt is used as a quick and efficient means, usually by family members, to fulfill their cultural expectations. Although every nationality has its own spin on how to wield the guilt sword, the ramifications are the same: You blame yourself for not living up to the expectations of family, and then you get clobbered by **cultural guilt**.

Here's a story about Belinda, a newlywed who married into a culture she knew very little about. One day she was on the phone with a friend, and simultaneously her mother-in-law called on the other line. Belinda told her mother-in-law she'd call her right back as she was just wrapping up another conversation. In a defeated and victimized tone, her mother-in-law shallowly uttered, "Oh, okay. ... I'll go away. ... Maybe call me some other time." She closed the conversation with a huge woe-is-me sigh and a poignant click. Good grief! Suddenly Belinda felt immense guilt because of her mother-in-law's victimized tone. Had she said something wrong? Although Belinda had no ill intent, the Guilt Monster glared sternly down its nose at her, insinuating she'd just blown off her dear sweet mother-in-law.

Belinda discussed the event with her husband. He told her that in their culture it is disrespectful to put an elderly family member "on hold." The needs of family always come before the needs of all others. Belinda had no idea of these unspoken cultural rules, but felt a tsunami of **cultural guilt** slam her to the ground nonetheless.

Belinda eventually began to understand the cultural expectations of her husband's family and has since learned to keep their beliefs well in mind to avoid future miscommunication. However, she made it clear to her husband that she was not going to change her way of life just to accommodate his mother's strict cultural expectations. She has learned to gently deflect her mother-in-law's guilt torpedoes by not taking her judgemental reactions personally.

We each have our own cultural expectations, and each of us holds them at different degrees of importance. When someone insinuates you are shameful for not living up to their cultural demands, it is best to communicate that it was not your intent to harm or disrespect, you were simply not privy to their cultural norms. As well, you may not be interested in living under the same set of cultural rules as others; therefore, do not allow **cultural guilt** to sway you into being someone you are not comfortable with!

A colleague of mine shared a story about the debilitating rush of **cultural guilt** she received from her parents every time she did not agree to partake in certain religious ceremonies. "I did it for my mom and dad, and you should do the same for me" is a phrase her parents often used as a means to an end. These cultural expectations easily get passed down from one generation to the next out of sheer habit. **Cultural guilt** must be identified and understood if you are to eradicate the emotional battering you feel at its hands. Instead of getting sucker punched by the Guilt Monster, protect yourself with boundaries and open communication. Although you may continue to disappoint certain family members for not fulfilling your supposed cultural duty, it is YOUR life to live as you choose, and no one has a right to make you feel guilty. Do not allow the Guilt Monster to turn you into chopped liver because you do not believe in the same cultural beliefs as others, in particular family.

There will be upheavals in every culture as customs alter or fade with each new generation. In order for older generations to maintain their customs, they often use fear and guilt as tools to maintain the status quo. You can easily get guilted into family dinners, religious traditions, marital customs, etc. if you are not aware of your boundaries. Some of these customs are antiquated, and some are considered cruel and sexist such as child marriages or gender inequality. Cultural expectations can be wonderful as long as you have given your participation some thought and are in agreement. If, however, you are not in agreement, and find you are uncomfortable with what they stand for, you should never allow guilt to be the by-product of your decision.

The Guilt Monster will have a full-fledged temper tantrum if you display any signs of individuality or evolution by pulling away from cultural expectations, such as living together versus being married, not having children versus having a family, and not celebrating every cultural holiday, just to name a few. You have every right to live within the boundaries you feel most comfortable. Although you are unable to fulfill another's deep-rooted cultural expectation at every turn, express your love and respect towards them, but be clear that you want to live YOUR life YOUR way. As you gradually become more confident in breaking free from certain cultural norms, the Guilt Monster's thunderous roar will eventually turn to a growl and finally a mere whimper as you become more empowered and your **cultural guilt** begins to fade. Always be proud of your cultural roots; just don't allow the Guilt Monster to take root in you.

12 DATING GUILT

*When you feel guilty about not
satisfying your date's expectations*

DATING GUILT **CAN EASILY BLUR** your boundaries after just
one date, a series of dates, or a long-term dating situation.
It manifests when you don't feel you are living up to your
date's expectations, and you begin to wonder if you are
somehow to blame. You dismiss the warning signs from
your intuition that your boundaries are not being taken
seriously, and allow yourself to get reeled into fulfilling
your date's wishes. There is no need to walk the plank
of shame for voicing your opinion and protecting your
boundaries. You are in charge of your decisions, so do
not allow your date to talk you into anything you are not
comfortable with. When you feel it's time to stop dating
someone because you begin to see hairline cracks in his or
her character and your boundaries are not being honored,
please do not blame yourself for bursting that person's
love bubble. Be as gentle as possible in executing your exit
strategy, but if you must be firm to get your point across,
so be it! All is fair in love and war. The other person's

feelings are important, but they are never as important as yours! Blaming yourself for how your date reacts to your decisions is not your burden to bear; therefore, there is no need to feel the onslaught of **dating guilt**.

When you have entered the dating arena—whether it's online dating, speed dating, a blind date, or any other type of dating—the key word to focus on is *dating*. You are not exclusive with, necessarily sleeping with, or loyal to anyone; you are a free agent testing the waters of love. Dating is simply getting to know someone at your own pace with the help of stimulating conversation, dinners, movies, walks along the beach, etc. While dating and having fun, you are also observing the evolution of the relationship, and deciding whether is serves you well, therefore guilt should never enter the equation when there are matters to discuss. Guilt is a form of manipulation, and you must be vigilant of it being utilised to blur your boundaries.

If the person you are dating makes you feel guilty for not having sex, not being available every waking minute, or not agreeing with them on particular matters, then those are red flags. When red flags start popping up, so should your boundary's antenna. Be on high alert to any unsavory patterns of behavior, and beware of doling out second, third and fourth chances to recurring issues; this will never serve you well if change is not occuring. As well, it is highly unlikely your date is taking you seriously if they don't "get it" the first time you mention your concerns. Hearing a lot of empty promises and idle talk, with no accompanied action to respect your wishes, is yet another neon red flag.

If your date is not taking you seriously or making you feel bad, your dating time with him or her is most likely O-V-E-R. Speaking your mind, ending a date early, or deciding to no longer date someone, is nothing to feel guilty about. Most likely you've outgrown your date and it is time to part ways. It is better to end the date (albeit with an explanation like "I don't feel we have enough in common") than to prolong the agony of being with someone you aren't comfortable with, have zero in common with, or that continues to disrespect and disappoint you. Besides, you don't want to give your date false hope by continuing to see him or her, when you know in your heart your relationship is not going to flourish. Actually, you are doing the person a favor by calling it off. Why feel **dating guilt** about expecting the best for yourself and living in truth?

After many dates, if exclusivity and a future with someone is what you're after, don't assume that it's also your partner's desire. The other person may only be interested in a relationship without a formal commitment. Perhaps the person has no clue whatsoever what he or she wants. In any case, do not allow the Guilt Monster to Gorilla Glue your lips together for fear of hurting the other person's feelings due to voicing your relationship goals.

Communicate your needs often in order not to waste valuable time and later find yourself swimming in a sea of regret and disappointment. If you plan to live your life one way and your date has opposing plans, most likely you are NOT going to be compatible long term. If a serious, forever relationship is your ultimate landing point, consider bailing out if your sweetie is not making any firm long-term plans that include you. Is he or she talking about your future together? Is there an engagement ring? Are you buying a place together? In order for a relationship to sustain itself, both parties must continue to remain fulfilled and there should be continued forward movement in its evolution.

It's YOUR life, and you have every right to express your innermost thoughts and desires when dating. Don't waste your precious time (a commodity you can never buy back) expecting a commitment only to be horrified years down the line that you're not part of your date's master plan. If your relationship has become stagnant and has failed to grow, then it's time to move on and find the future you are looking for.

Not being on the same page with a long-term date has the power to chisel away at your inner joy. If your needs are not addressed, you may become bitter, resentful, angry and sad. This is emotionally toxic and, if left unchecked, may affect your physical and mental health. Cut your losses by ending the relationship, and seek someone who is more like-minded. Wriggle out of the Guilt Monster's suffocating love nest, and breathe the fresh air of new possibilities. Believe unequivocally in getting what you want and deserve from each and every relationship.

While waiting for Mr. or Miss Right to appear, write down some things you require of a partner so you'll be fully aware of such a person when he or she comes your way. Continue to have faith in the relationship fairy, knowing that eventually the right person will come along to fulfill your dreams. If you don't believe in fairies, there's always online dating!

Regarding the sex/intimacy part of the dating equation, this must be mutual to both parties involved. Both parties should be in agreement with this escalation in the relationship. In my opinion, as soon as sex enters the equation, usually one of the parties feels it is now "official" that they are a committed couple. Avoid possible disappointment by knowing this is not always the case. When dating, take nothing for granted; ask questions often in order to always know where you stand. Some people consider having sex very sacred, whereas others are cavalier about it. It is important to communicate your desires in order to protect your boundaries. As well, if you have been on several dates and are NOT ready to dive into the sheets, never feel you *owe* your date that pleasure. Not wanting to satisfy your date's physical appetite is nothing to feel guilty about. Be upfront regarding your feelings and comfort zone at all times. This will be less arduous if you never allow the Guilt Monster to be your chaperone.

Some may find my advice rather old school and antiquated, but one thing that will never change—no matter where we land in history or what religion we believe or don't believe—is that we all have feelings. And feelings must be acknowledged, nurtured, articulated, protected and respected. Do not be a contestant on *The Dating Game* where the Guilt Monster is behind door number one, two, and three anxiously awaiting to be chosen in order to manipulate or dissappoint you! I have found that one party, if not both, eventually gets hurt if the dating boundaries are not communicated and respect is not maintained. Protect your beautiful body and soul when dating. If you encounter red flags, you should take them seriously, because one red flag is always one too many!

By respecting your boundaries, you will avoid a lot of emotional pain. If temporary loneliness ensues because of a breakup resulting from being true to yourself, know that it's well worth the wait to find a like-minded mate. In the end your soul will breathe a sigh of relief instead of a gasp of regret.

As you snuggle on the couch with your date, make certain the Guilt Monster isn't squeezed between the two of you for some manipulative third-rate pillow talk.

13 DEATH GUILT

When you feel guilty about not having another opportunity to express your sentiments with a deceased loved one

DEATH. **THE WORD ITSELF AROUSES** feelings of doom, gloom, and heartache. It's a heavy and somber word that most don't want to hear and would rather avoid. When you experience **death guilt**, it is usually because you no longer have the opportunity to forgive, apologize, or express your innermost thoughts to the deceased. Your emotions have the potential to plunge into a vast sea of darkness because you've run out of chances to convey your feelings to someone. Initially you blame yourself, then you feel remorseful, and lastly you cover your disappointment in a weighted blanket of guilt. This is all unnecessary, as no one knows when their last moments with a loved one will be, and no one is aware of how their emotions will reveal themselves when that moment arrives.

A friend's father was in the hospital and had only days to live. My friend would visit him for hours each day, hoping they could share a few heartfelt last words, but his dad was always unconscious. On one occasion, his sister went to visit their father, and during a short-lived lucid moment he told his daughter, "I love you." The next day, my friend eagerly returned to the hospital hoping his father would utter those same precious words to him as well, but once again his father was unresponsive.

The following day his father died, leaving my friend in a straitjacket of grief. Not only did he have to deal with the emotional toll from his dad's death, but also the guilt about having missed the last opportunity to tell his father he loved him; words neither of them ever shared. In the past, my friend and his father were always very guarded about their feelings; it was simply not in their nature to share deep emotions. Although my friend knew his dad loved him, in all his life the words *I love you* had never graced his ears.

I tried to comfort my visibly distraught friend by telling him it was not too late to share his feelings of love with his father. I urged him to find a quiet spot and talk to his dad in prayer, or visit his burial site and share his sentiments. "It's not the same," he exclaimed. "He's not here *now*! I will never, ever have the opportunity to look into my dad's eyes and tell him I love him."

The Guilt Monster had put my friend's heart in a choke hold, blaming him for not addressing the situation sooner. After living with **death guilt** for years, my friend finally made peace with himself, and the guilt dissipated as he realized his negative thoughts from the past were infringing on his joy in the present. Now he is well aware of how important it is for him to verbally express his love to those special people in his life. He has learned a valuable lesson about his inner workings, and instead of feeling **death guilt**, he is thankful for being enlightened to the importance of expressing his love to others.

I don't believe any deceased person would want their loved ones carrying the burden of self-imposed guilt. They would definitely want their loved ones to extinguish the roaring flames of their guilty conscience and carry on unencumbered with the precious gift of life. My friend's experience with his father should be looked upon as a positive, because it taught him how important it is to verbalize his love. Sometimes, the importance of certain matters remains dormant until something awakens them within you. Only then do you realize their true significance.

Another story that comes to mind revolves around a woman I'll call Lidia. Her sister was admitted to the hospital for emergency heart surgery. As it turned out, the operation was successful, but soon afterward, she developed an infection and died from complications. The Guilt Monster gave Lidia a severe shakedown because immediately after her sister's operation, she'd gotten into an argument with her. Before it got resolved, her sister unexpectedly died. Lidia was not only heartbroken about her sister's death, but also numb with guilt for having allowed anger to fill her last precious words to her.

When **death guilt** takes over your thoughts, it's easy to become emotionally paralyzed. You feel unworthy of future happiness because of a less than perfect ending with a loved one. With no further opportunities to express yourself, or right the wrong, you decide that the awaiting arms of the Guilt Monster should remain your only comfort.

Although Lidia did not wish her last words to her sister to be harsh, she suffered the wrath of that final conversation nonetheless. Lidia felt heartbroken that she was unable to make amends with her sister before she died, and deserved to live in nothing more than misery. I suggested making peace with her sister through meditation and prayer. I reminded Lidia that it was not her *intent* to have her last words to her sister be angry ones, and even if it was, it was in her best interests to learn from the experience and release her burden through self-forgiveness.

When someone dies with whom you feel you have unfinished business, realize that life doesn't always allow for fairy-tale endings. Own your actions in order to feel the fullness of your emotions, learn from the scenario, then release the manufactured guilt from your being. I believe that it is healthy to *own* your guilt and grieve, but it is equally beneficial to forgive yourself for your imperfections or oversights and release all negative thoughts. Self-discovery can be a painful process, so please be gentle with yourself along the way. Allow your soul the space to breathe the air of enlightenment, and through this renewal and the knowledge you have obtained, continue your journey unencumbered by guilt.

Death guilt may also be experienced when you ponder if you were amply available for your dearly departed during his or her moments of need. Your obsessive thoughts of your supposed shortcomings give the Guilt Monster a great deal of ammunition to use against you. You ask questions of yourself such as, "Did I do my duty as a daughter [or son, friend, coworker, neighbor, etc.] while [the deceased] was alive?" You wonder if you visited enough, encouraged enough, and loved enough. Unfortunately, death does not allow for any rewinding of the tape or dress rehearsals; therefore, you must understand that you did your best at that particular time, with the knowledge and foresight you had. If you feel you could have done more, then grow from the experience and do more for others in the future—minus the Guilt Monster wiping away your river of tears with its oversized hankie of remorse.

Break the toxic habit of condemning yourself with **death guilt**, and instead be thankful for becoming enlightened. Learn to live each day more conscious of the power of your words and deeds while the opportunity is available. Instead of allowing the Guilt Monster to be your film projectionist, replaying your regretful past over and over again, move onward and upward by playing your mind's new movie entitled, "Love, Enlightenment, and Forgiveness."

14 DECISION GUILT

When you feel guilty because your decisions didn't please others

DECISIONS, DECISIONS, DECISIONS! WHAT TO do, when to do it, where to do it? Argh! You finally make a decision about when and where to have your wedding, but some family members are not thrilled about your plans, and you feel the Guilt Monster breathing heavily down your tiara! The Guilt Monster can't believe how selfish you are by having selected a destination wedding instead of pleasing your parents and getting married at home. Due to disappointing your parents, you feel you deserve to have your dream wedding blown up into a million pieces by the Guilt Monster's cruise missle of shame.

In reality, it is YOUR wedding; therefore, the decision should be yours. You have every right to celebrate it where you desire. As with most decisions, it is important to weigh all the variables before you land on a final resolution. However, with every decision, there is a high probability you may upset someone that has other ideas or expectations that do not agree with yours. This has the potential to cause friction and upset others, leaving you with a heavy dose of **decision guilt**. Not to worry, because opinions regarding decisions are wide-ranging, making it humanly impossible to please everyone. It is wise, however, to keep an open mind when making a decision that involves others, as their ideas may shed light on variables you overlooked or were unaware of. This added input may change your final outcome. Knowledge is power, so accumulate as much information as you can from reliable sources before making an executive decision. In the end, however, the *final* decision is yours, right down to the number of beads on your wedding gown.

If those who try to sway your decisions get aggressive and start tag-teaming with the Guilt Monster, you have to stand firm in your convictions so they understand you mean business! Often, friends and family can give the impression that they know what's best for you, especially if you are a people pleaser or not in the habit of expressing your opinion. Write down all the pros and cons of the situation in question, and review this list regularly before chiseling your final decision in stone.

When you demand that the Guilt Monster no longer stands on your wedding train, you will be able to move freely and make wise decisions with the utmost clarity. Do not get swayed into decisions that are not supportive of what you truly want, as this will only plant the seed of resentment within you towards others. Believe in your well-rounded decisions as they are a reflection of your uniqueness. The next time the Guilt Monster tailgates your decision-making, put your boundaries in turbo thrust and leave the beast in a plume of dust.

15 DELEGATION GUILT

When you feel guilty about allocating your tasks to another

SOMEWHERE ALONG LIFE'S WAY, I came to the conclusion that delegating my duties signified I was one of the following: not up to the challenge, lazy, unintelligent, or a failure. I just didn't feel worthy of receiving any outside help. I'm not sure where this defeatist mind-set originated, but it is definitely not a great way to go through life. I forever equated *delegating* as a weakness instead of a strength, and decided weakness is an undesirable trait worthy of punishment. My punishment of choice was none other than guilt.

I've since come to realize we are not machines, and are not intended to do everything brilliantly, all the time, all by our little lonesomes. As it turns out, successful people delegate tasks frequently to free up valuable time for other matters. Richard Branson is an excellent example of this. He starts a new company and finds someone else to run it so he can focus on his next project or, heck, take a well-deserved vacation. Whatever the reason, never feel

delegation guilt in order to free up time, conserve energy, and get the job done! Thankfully, I have friends who are kings and queens of delegating, and they have helped me pave the way to becoming an expert.

When I went grocery shopping recently at one of the big-box stores that do not bag your groceries, I got cranky and anxious. Not only did I have to shop for my elderly parents, my children, and myself, but I also had to bag the groceries with the little energy I had left after a long day. Wasn't pushing the overflowing cart through the aisles while dodging screaming kids and aisle loiterers (people who mindlessly block the aisle with their carts while they decide what they want to buy) enough?

One day I vented to my friend about my horrific shopping experiences. I mentioned that I detested bagging my own groceries, and if I didn't bag them fast enough, the cashier had to slow down the conveyer belt, which in turn invited a glare of doom from others waiting impatiently in line, directed towards me. At this point my anxiety kicked in at full throttle. I asked my friend if she ever felt as overwhelmed while grocery shopping as I did. Her answer was quite simple: "I never have that problem because I *ask* the cashier to find an employee to bag the groceries for me."

What?! "You asked an employee to do it for you?" I'd never even considered that to be an option. Needless to say, from that day forward I asked the cashier for some much-needed assistance and never again received the glares of doom for my tardy *bagging* execution. Now I exit the store with a smile on my face and a hop in my step. Cost of delegating? There is no cost, only profit, as you learn how to conserve energy and feel more empowered! A win-win situation.

Thankfully, I no longer wear the hat of a single-parent victim, struggling like a battered ping-pong ball as I shuttle back and forth with the endless dispensing and bagging of groceries. My delegating skills have grown, and instead of trying to do everything myself and living in a state of perpetual exhaustion, I have learned to delegate duties and free up valuable time and energy for more enjoyable activities.

If I have no time to clean the house, I ask my daughters to help, call an agency, or leave my chores for another day until I am in the frame of mind to take it on. If I don't have time to fix my computer or don't know how, I call a friend or neighbor to do it for me. If I don't have time to cook dinner, there are several services that will deliver a hot meal right to my door. Delegating creates more balance in my life, and the extra free time has made me a lot happier. I have released the ball and chain of **delegation guilt** in exchange for more freedom, simply by reaching out and obtaining help. The Guilt Monster will never again make me feel unworthy of asking for assistance while simultaneously swatting me with a rolled-up gossip magazine in the hopes that I'll bag my groceries faster.

Another delegating scenario took place when I decided to paint my house and developed carpal tunnel syndrome. My boyfriend told me I should not be doing that kind of work because I already had many more pressing duties on my plate, such as raising my daughters, working full time, spending a day or two a week helping my parents, and visiting my autistic brother out of town. To add fuel to the fire, I was on a tight budget, so hiring a painter was completely out of the question! My boyfriend, however, offered to pay for a professional painter and housekeeper to make my life easier. Now you're probably thinking, *How fortuitous*, but I refused the money, thinking I should take care of everything myself. Why, you ask? **Delegation guilt!**

I felt unworthy of accepting help because I believed painting my house was solely *my* responsibility and not my boyfriend's. Although his money was offered in a loving manner, I was unable to graciously accept it. I stubbornly pushed myself to the point of exhaustion, while my boyfriend stood by and watched me wear myself out in silent agony. Then one day, while painting, my aching hands and shoulders started screaming at me, and I had an epiphany. *Why in the heck am I wearing out my body, mind and soul when there are so many other more pleasant things I'd rather be doing?* I promptly picked up the phone and hired a professional painter. I decided I would temporarily cut back on other expenses in order to make it financially feasible. I called my boyfriend and told him the good news. He was thrilled at my decision and said he would help me with the bill and we would celebrate. I thanked him for planting in me the seed of *delegating* and for being patient while I figured out how to change my thinking and do away with my debilitating, manufactured guilt. Unfortunately, it took a lot of aches and pains to learn my lesson, but I implore you, take my advice and start delegating ASAP. Just try it once or twice and see how relieved you feel doing away with a chore or two. I've since learned to be proactive and delegate duties sooner rather than later, instead of waiting until I am frustrated, miserable and completely out of steam.

As it turned out, my boyfriend was also dealing with some **delegating guilt** of his own. He runs a large company and felt guilty if he didn't have his hands in every pie, from buying the ingredients, mixing, chopping, grating, rolling, and baking every account. I'm not saying he shouldn't oversee his operations, but there is only so much one person can handle before they become resentful. I told him he was developing anxiety and frustration because of his intense workload and mentioned that he might want to delegate some of his duties to his underlings or hire extra help.

Initially he felt it was a poor reflection of his capabilities if he couldn't control every nuance of every account, but eventually he gave my advice a whirl. He has since developed a sweet tooth for delegating and now has extra time on his hands to relax, socialize, and travel: an excellent recipe for happiness. It is wise to delegate duties in order to create more time in your life to enjoy an extra long lunch, instead of feeling like an overcooked noodle in the Guilt Monster's ramen.

16 DISCIPLINE GUILT

When you feel guilty about enforcing rules to correct your child's disobedience

JUST THE OTHER DAY, ALL hell broke loose at the home of my dear friend Andrea. She is raising two daughters as a single parent. Oftentimes, Andrea works long hours and is not always available to observe and discipline her children's behavior. When she returns from work and her daughters are behaving badly, she enforces the rules, but then feels **discipline guilt** because she thinks it gives her children the impression that her only role with them is that of a disciplinarian.

Her daughters are fifteen and seventeen, and the teen years are well known for voicing one's independence by testing the parameters of rules both inside and outside the home. If parents do not instill strict rules, because they fear losing the bond with their children, they may create in them a runaway train of bad behavior. This was the case with Andrea. She knew she had to change her tactics immediately before matters went from bad to worse.

Andrea decided to have her daughters stay with her mother for a few days in order to collect her thoughts and seek outside advice. When her daughters were told of the plan to move in with their grandma, they were obstinate and refused to go. They immediately got dressed and bolted out the door. Thankfully, Andrea's mom saw her grandchildren at the bus stop before arriving and convinced them to get in the car. She then drove to Andrea's and collected a suitcase with enough clothing for a few days. Now, some people may find this form of discipline over the top; however, this mom was at her wits' end, near a breakdown and desperate for a respite. She needed some solitude in order to regain clarity and find a solution to bring harmony back into the home.

As it turned out, the girls came home after school the next day instead of spending the extra night at their grandmother's. When they entered the front door, Andrea was there to greet them, and they were as defiant as ever. Andrea, with her new rules firmly in place, said they were welcome to stay, but they were grounded for their previous bad behavior and for not staying at their grandmother's house for the planned duration. Although Andrea was trying her best to change her old habits and enforce strict rules, as recommended by her friends and professionals, her daughters did not take her seriously. They knew from past experience that eventually their mom would give up and give in, and they could carry on as they pleased. Their reply to their mother was "Look, Mommy dearest, we're only here to take a shower, make a few calls, and collect more clothes, and we'll be outta here."

At that point, Andrea stood firm and informed them that they had just ten minutes to collect their belongings before returning to their grandmother's. She also said they were not allowed to use the shower. "When you are disrespectful to me, you lose all privileges, and that includes use of the shower," she exclaimed. Andrea's new boundaries were set in stone, and although she felt the presence of the Guilt Monster closing in on her with every disciplinary word, she stood resolute.

A few minutes later, as her kids were going out the door, Andrea suddenly felt waves of guilt come out of nowhere and sweep her and her strict rules out to sea. She began to second-guess her newfound disciplinary tactics and wondered if she had driven an even deeper wedge between herself and her daughters. After her children left, she rested her head on the Guilt Monster's massive shoulder, crying a river that was easily absorbed by his mangy blue coat. Andrea felt she was solely to blame for her children's poor behavior due to: being a single parent, having to occasionally work out of town, not having her boundaries firmly in place, and at times losing her temper. **Discipine guilt** was having a field day in Andrea's mind! Although she had finally decided to enforce the house rules with her daughters, it was going to take them some time to realize the new rules were there to stay, and that respecting their mom was to become the new normal.

With every learning curve, there is always a time of transition before change firmly takes hold. Andrea was in transition as well, wondering if her daughters would eventually accept the new house rules and reestablish a loving bond with her. For the moment, however, Andrea's habitual guilty feelings resurfaced and the Guilt Monster wiped away her river of tears, gave her a big hug, and poured her another dirty martini.

The last thing Andrea should have been doing was cozying up to the Guilt Monster when she was trying to discipline her children and instill proper family values. She was trying her best to teach her children about respect, and she absolutely, unequivocally had no reason to feel guilty about it. The next time Andrea reinforced her new house rules, she ushered the Guilt Monster out the door and did not require a martini or any other alcoholic beverage. This is a story about tough love! One should not feel an iota of guilt about enforcing rules and disciplining bad behaviour to create respect and harmony in the home, as long as it is done in the spirit of love.

Tranquility eventually returned to Andrea's home as her children began to understand that the new rules and discipline for poor behavior were here to stay. It is normal for all children to test their boundaries; that's how they learn the difference between right and wrong. That is why it is important to regularly discuss the implementation of rules and why they are so important to follow.

Instead of taking an ice-cold guilt shower when you reinforce the rules, you should feel sun-kissed that you are doing your children a huge service by teaching them how to be respectful and decent people. It is advantageous for your children to learn lessons at home, where they can be monitored in a safe environment and issues can be easily rectified, instead of them possibly paying a huge penalty for indiscretions far from the protection of their parents.

Children must realize life has many lessons, and respecting others is definitely on the short list. If rules are broken and your children will not listen to reason, action is necessary to make them aware that there are repercussions for bad behavior. Loss of privileges is always a great place to start. If you are not sure how to discipline your children, I recommend reading Barbara Coloroso's books on child-rearing or a plethora of other books on the subject, coupled with advice from a counselor, friends, and family.

In closing, if you weren't strict on addressing your child's poor behavior when he or she was younger, don't blame yourself for not having been privy to superior child-rearing methods earlier. It's never too late to start enforcing new rules. Be patient, understanding, and communicative with your children as they adjust to your newfound expectations of them. When tough love is a must, the Guilt Monster you should never trust.

17 DIVORCE GUILT

*When you feel guilty for having
caused emotional pain to others
because you have chosen to divorce*

MY FRIEND RACHEL CAME OVER for lunch the other day with a bottle of wine in one hand and a bomb to drop in the other. I was blindsided when she told me she was about to serve her husband with divorce papers. Her husband had moved out a few weeks ago, and her children were having difficulty adjusting. She went on to say her twelve-year-old daughter had been asked by her English teacher to write a story about her family and what she would change about it if she could. Her one wish was to see her mom and dad get back together so they could be a family again. Heartbreak Alley? You bet! My friend, immediately hit by a bolt of **divorce guilt** for being the cause of her daughter's heartbreak, cried buckets of guilt-infused tears into her already brimming wineglass.

I tried to comfort my friend by sharing the story of *my* divorce, which took place when my daughters were eight. At that time, my children also wanted their family back together, as would any child. Now that they are older, they have come to realize some of the reasons why the divorce took place. They have since made comments such as "You two are like night and day" and are now able to laugh about it.

When two people grow apart and have little in common and/or disrespect each other, it becomes emotionally unhealthy for all involved and makes it increasingly difficult to continue living under the same roof. Moreover, it sets a poor example for children as to the ingredients needed for a happy home. As a parent, I felt it was my duty to get a divorce in order to protect my children from emotional dysfunction. Initially I felt guilty for divorcing my children's father, but I had to look at the big picture and protect them from an unhappy and unstable environment. Now that time has passed, I know I did the right thing as we are all happier, their father included.

After seeking a divorce, you may experience **divorce guilt** because you feel responsible for hurting everyone's feelings, including those of your parents, your children, and other family members and friends. However, these people's negative reaction to your divorce should not fall squarely on your shoulders when all you are trying to do is reclaim some sense of normalcy and joy. Reactions will differ greatly; therefore, be patient and understanding toward everyone involved as they process the event. I assure you they will adjust over time and find a way to come to terms with your decision. However, if they remain discontent, that is solely *their* choice, out of your control, and their responsibility to deal with. The Guilt Monster should never be allowed a seat at your divorce lawyer's boardroom table.

Before following through on a divorce, you may ask yourself if you could have loved more, been in better shape, been more accommodating, bought more flowers, etc. Once you have taken a hard look at why divorce is the only solution left standing that will eradicate abuse, misery, infidelity, or an emotional void, why feel guilty? If it is emotionally and physically healing—and for the greater good of yourself and your family—then you're doing the right thing. Naturally, your decision will cause some hurt, disappointment and sadness, but given time, the heart and mind will heal and happier times will prevail. Change is difficult at the best of times, as most of us prefer to live in familiar situations. It makes us feel safe and in control. Unfortunately, change is a constant in life, and sometimes change is for the best. Instead of allowing **divorce guilt** to perpetually *drain* your happiness account, it would be more fitting to flush the Guilt Monster down the *drain*.

In order to heal from the aftermath of a divorce, it is important to keep the lines of communication open with your children, the ex if possible, and family members and friends. Supply your children with age appropriate reasons why you had to leave the marriage, so they have some understanding of the situation. Also, do your best never to degrade your soon-to-be ex within your child's earshot, even if he or she deserves that and so much more. In a child's eyes, no matter how poorly Mom or Dad has behaved, there is usually a special place tucked away in their hearts just for them; please respect the fragility of their feelings.

In the case of my friend reading about the sadness of divorce in her daughter's letter, I advised her to talk to her daughter openly. I suggested she comfort and reassure her that all would be well no matter what, and she would always remain their special little girl. I also recommended that my friend make it clear to her daughter that her dad would always be her *real* dad, and no one would ever take his place. Children are sensitive, so please put aside your anger, resentment, and any other negative emotions toward your ex while in their presence. Constantly reassure your children that the divorce has absolutely nothing to do with them, or your soon-to-be ex's love of them. If you feel they may need councilling to overcome this emotional hurdle, find a professional they are comfortable with and can relate to.

When your marriage has reached the point of filing for divorce, it is probably for the best. No one wants to live in a home filled with neglect, abuse, or sadness, and no parent wants their children thinking that such a dynamic is normal. There are plenty of books and outside help to walk you through the healing steps that follow a divorce. Use them! Initially, focus on your healing by spending quality time with your family and friends. Have faith in happier, fulfilling, and more peaceful tomorrows, and leave the past where it belongs: in the past. Your world will continue to blossom after walking down the icy corridors of divorce court, and your dormant effervescence will eventually bubble to the surface once again. Court and the Guilt Monster are dismissed!

18 DNA GUILT

*When you feel guilty because it's
part of your genetic makeup*

DNA IS THE CARRIER OF your genetic information, pulsating messages to every part of your body and mind. Some of the reasons you feel pangs of guilt for no apparent reason have to do with how you react on a cellular level. My theory is that generations of "guilt conditioning" reside in your DNA. Because DNA holds your genetic information, it is a template for how you process information. Do you always feel guilty for no reason? Are you perpetually looking over your shoulder, wondering when the axe of guilt will stealthily fall upon you, judging your every move, slicing and dicing your self-esteem, freedom of speech, and overall emotional wellness? If so, you are long overdue to start obliterating eons of **DNA guilt**.

My friend's daughter was fortunate enough to receive a beautiful house for her thirty-first birthday, bought and paid for by her grandmother. After experiencing the initial high of getting such a generous gift, her emotions quickly nosedived into the awaiting arms of the Guilt Monster.

My friend couldn't figure out why her daughter felt guilty? "I didn't raise her to feel guilty about anything," she said. I told her that sometimes we feel guilty for no reason and it is just part of our overall makeup.

There is, however, a way to reverse **DNA guilt** through the practice of meditation and being mindful every time you feel unworthy. You must train yourself to be hyperaware when you feel even a smattering of guilt. Immediately ask yourself what is prompting you to feel this way. Is it substantiated because you have committed a criminal offense or a premeditated misdeed? If you answer no to these questions, then your guilt is manufactured and completely unnecessary.

Identify your negative feelings associated with guilt, and replace them with their opposites. For example, instead of feeling guilty, feel blameless. Instead of feeling unworthy, feel deserving. For every negative feeling that floats through your mind, immediately find its polar opposite and meditate on it—feel the warm change within yourself as you release the guilt within, and note how your body and mind become less agitated and tense. Keep a record of your findings. Review them often. Focus on releasing antiquated, habitual, and toxic guilt messaging from your system.

Each *guilt transaction* you allow to seep into your thoughts adds another fortifying coat of guilt to your DNA and another feather in the cap of the Guilt Monster. Be on high alert, particularly in the presence of *guilt taskmasters.* Guilt taskmasters utilize guilt, consciously or otherwise, as a means to control others. Usually those who are hyper sensitive and compassionate are prime targets. Because of your compassionate nature, it's instinctive to want to oblige others; however, the more you're sucked into the guilt taskmasters'demands, the more you will fortify the guilt sequencing in your DNA.

Eliminating guilt from your DNA will not happen in the blink of an eye, but with practice, patience, awareness, and meditation, you will succeed. Do yourself the favor of releasing your paralyzing guilt conditioning, and banish the sludgy Guilt Monster from sliding around freely on your deserving and gleaming strands of DNA.

19 DONATION GUILT

*When you feel guilty about
your donation contribution*

AH, THE ANGEL SITTING PEACEFULLY on your right shoulder says you provided adequately to your favorite charity, but the Guilt Monster jumping up and down on your left shoulder and wearing out your rotator cuff, is screaming that you are a cheap, inconsiderate so-and-so and must donate more! You consider yourself a giving person but always manage to second-guess if your donation was adequate. This topic is a no-brainer for the Guilt Monster to work its magic. Without much effort, it reopens your wallet, finds a credit card, and donates more money than your budget can safely accommodate.

Charities are many and far reaching, from big names like the United Way and Red Cross to your neighbor's basketball team, your husband's work fundraiser, and your daughter's son's friend's field hockey team. Get my drift? It's endless. I believe in giving; however, you must discern the amount that is reasonable and affordable. Be realistic, leaving enough in your bank account to maintain a balanced budget.

I was watching an episode of *Till Debt Do You Part*, a television series that teaches the nuances of balancing your budget and getting out of debt. Although the woman on the show was horrendously in debt, she continued to donate approximately $400 a month to several charities. This show of generosity made it clear that she had a great deal of compassion; however, it is not a wise allocation of funds when the interest on your credit card far exceeds your charitable donations. The woman in debt mentioned she felt guilty if she did not contribute to others who were less fortunate. Upon hearing this, the counselor on the show pointed out that the woman was ironically heading in the same financial direction of those she was so eager to help. Soon she wouldn't be able to assist anyone because her credit score was in a perpetual free fall. If something wasn't done quickly to rescue her finances, not only would she be unable to donate to her favorite charities but she would be in need of charitable assistance herself. Yikes! She wasn't thinking straight because she was obtaining poor financial advice from her overbearing accountant, namely the Guilt Monster.

The counselor's first strategic move was to have all charitable donations come to a screeching halt. Next, she put many other items on the chopping block, including dining out, shopping, sports events, concerts, and vacations, until Ms. Spendthrift got a realistic view of how to live within her means and bring her checkbook back into the black. After her finances got an overhaul and were above water, she learned to become aware of keeping the Guilt Monster's paws away from her overused wallet. Eventually this woman figured out how to spend within her means and resumed donating to her favorite charities without blowing her budget.

The Guilt Monster also loves to exercise its donation manipulation in the aftermath of a natural disaster. It knows such situations tug at one's sympathies; therefore, you become an easy target. The 2004 tsunami in Asia brought this to the forefront for me. I was so touched by that tragedy that I immediately went online and donated. My parents were also emotionally impacted by the tsunami's aftermath and donated a larger sum than I did because they had the financial means to do so. In hindsight, I probably donated more than I felt comfortable with because I felt lucky being out of harm's way while others were suffering. Whenever you decide to donate, remain realistic about your budget, and keep guilt out of the equation.

To avoid the ramifications of **donation guilt**, donate with your head as well as your heart. Find a heart-mind balance. If your heart is screaming at you to donate, use the wise counsel of your mind to ask when and how much. It is possible to display compassion toward others and be prudent about your budget simultaneously.

Although my children do not have a lot of savings, they donate regularly within their financial comfort zone at animal rescue centers and various work-related charities. They do their part to gift within their means and do not suffer from **donation guilt** from offering the amount they are able. They realize that even the smallest effort can make a huge difference because money raised by charities is cumulative; it all adds up to a grand amount in the end. On one occasion, my daughters hoped to raise a few hundred dollars for Christmas gifts for the poor and ended up with an overwhelming $5,000 in donations. Your intent to donate is all that matters, not the amount.

If you are in the position of *asking* for a donation rather than giving, don't feel guilty thinking you are putting others on the spot. You are simply trying to do your part to help those less fortunate. It is up to the person you are asking to decide whether he or she wants to contribute. Raising money for worthwhile causes is a noble act; therefore, do not allow guilt to impede your charitable work. Most people are happy to help out, and it makes them feel good to do so. Both raising and donating money for charitable causes will make you feel like a hero, as long as the Guilt Monster doesn't take your cheque and add another zero.

20 ENJOYING-THE-MOMENT GUILT

Feeling guilty when you take the time to enjoy unplanned events

HAVE YOU EVER FELT GUILTY enjoying an unexpected lunch date, extra time walking through the park on a beautiful day, or talking to a neighbor for longer than expected, knowing you have a *kazillion* other things you should be doing? Although you thoroughly enjoyed these moments, in the back of your mind the Guilt Monster was pacing back and forth with its stopwatch, reminding you of your awaiting responsibilities. Instead of enjoying-the-moment, you are strung out on guilt because you think you are wasting time by not checking off more boxes on your to-do list. Also, you feel added guilt wondering if your mom is trying to reach you, the pets are lonely, the lawn needs mowing, or it's time to do something other than enjoy your special moment.

Although it is difficult at times to keep your life in balance, push the envelope and enjoy pleasant impromptu moments when they present themselves. This helps break up the demands of your premeditated day and allows for some soul-replenishing spontaneity and fun. Practice focusing only on the present moment instead of always drifting into your regimented future. Pleasant diversions are life's way of offering you a reprieve from the daily grind; be thankful. *Enjoying-the-moment* helps you recharge and reconnect with yourself and humanity. Embrace this space in time whether sharing your thoughts with others or getting lost in your own thoughts. Relinquish control once in a while and let the universe be in charge of pleasantly interrupting your busy schedule.

A friend called the other day asking me to join her for lunch at a *fancy-schmancy* restaurant. I immediately felt **enjoying-the-moment guilt** because I had not penned her into my already busy schedule. I tried sabotaging the invitation by asking her how much it would cost at *Fancyville*. It was my way of nixing the lunch date because I felt guilty about enjoying-the-moment. She replied, "Around a hundred dollars." *Around a hundred dollars? What! Are you kidding me?* Didn't she realize I was a single parent on a budget? I gracefully declined her proposal, but she quickly retorted that she would still love for me to join her and she would put the bill on her husband's account. With lunch paid for and no excuse not to attend other than having a bunch of boring chores to do, I continued to clobber myself with the Guilt Monster's overpriced baguette. My mind was so entrenched in completing my day as originally planned, that going out on a Tuesday afternoon for a lovely top-drawer lunch seemed counterintuitive and bordering on insanity.

I finally accepted the lunch invitation, but continued to sabotage myself out of habit. *I have nothing to wear. My hair isn't cooperating. I have too much to do. I don't deserve it. It's too cold out.* As I recall, this luncheon was not a threesome; my friend hadn't invited the Guilt Monster to join us as well. Needless to say, I finally pulled myself together and made it to lunch. My friend and I had a wonderful time sipping on mimosas, eating delicious food, laughing, and reminiscing. I realized I was having a spectacular time and feeling better than I had in a long while. I *enjoyed-the-moment* without placing any further limits or guilt on myself, and I had the most splendid three-and-a-half-hour lunch on record.

Allow your spirit room to be spontaneous and have fun. Learn to bring down your rigid walls of responsibility and go with the flow. When you learn to *enjoy-the-moment,* you will flambé the Guilt Monster clear out of your conscience and be able to savor every nuance of your crème brûlée.

21 FAMILY LOYALTY GUILT

When you feel guilty standing your ground with family members

YOUR IMMEDIATE AND EXTENDED FAMILY contains a diverse array of personalities and characters, some of which may rub you the wrong way. Some family members believe they have a right to cross the line in what they say and do with other family members because their behavior will not be questioned given the unwritten rule of *family loyalty*.

There are times when you want to give a family member a piece of your mind, but you restrain yourself to avoid causing any waves in your family circle. When you decide you can no longer keep silent and must express your true feelings, family members may frown at your actions. This is when **family loyalty guilt** takes hold. You have breached the unspoken family loyalty rule: Please family members no matter what! Being part of a family, you feel obligated to tolerate unsavory forms of behavior from certain relatives simply because you share the same family tree. However, when you decide to stand your ground because a family member crosses the line, the Guilt Monster will give your family tree a shake until the apples fall from its branches and rain down on your head.

I was getting a manicure the other day from a new aesthetician. She was so sweet, *sweet* being the operative word. She told me she was having problems again with her newly purchased vehicle. I told her to take it back to the dealership and trade it in for another car, adding that perhaps she had bought a lemon. She said she'd love to return it, but she'd bought it from her brother-in-law. Although she loathes him, she utilizes his dealership strictly because they are related, and she feels obligated. If she were to go elsewhere, she'd feel guilty for not supporting her extended family, not to mention dealing with the judgemental grumblings of other family members. As she continued to be unhappy about her car's performance, she eventually took it to a service station for an analysis, and the mechanic couldn't believe what a piece of garbage it was. He told her to take it back to the dealer and demand a refund. Needless to say, the aesthetician said it was out of the question because she had bought the vehicle from a family member and didn't want to create any family conflict.

This purchase was not the first but the second lemon she had acquired from her not-so-conscientious brother-in-law. Now you're probably saying, "Oh, cut the guy some slack; maybe they were both just lemons unbeknownst to him." The truth of the matter is, my manicurist found out from an independent mechanic that the repairs her brother-in-law claimed he had performed on her car were not done at all. As well, when she asked her brother-in-law to see the receipt for the work, he claimed he couldn't find it. Hmm, why did this young woman continue to disrespect herself by allowing the Guilt Monster to ride shotgun with her when buying a car? **Family loyalty guilt!**

I found out later that this frustrated young woman had finally suffered enough misery with the broken-down vehicles her brother-in-law repeatedly sold her, and at the risk of upsetting him and other family members, she became empowered enough to demand a full refund for her car. Did she feel vindicated? Yes! Did she feel **family loyalty guilt** after being repeatedly disrespected? Not this time! She had finally reached her boiling point after being repeatedly hurt, lied to, and taken advantage of. The lesson in this story is to not allow guilt to color your rational thought and cause you unnecessary grief. There is no reason to feel guilty when you are not getting respected or, in this case, receiving a proper product for your hard-earned money.

Manufactured **family loyalty guilt** no longer prevents this sweet young woman from expecting the respect she so rightfully deserves. There is no reason to give family members special treatment if they are out of line and blurring your personal boundaries. Find the courage to slam your trunk shut on out-of-line family members and **family loyalty guilt**. When family members are out of line, self-respect must win every time.

22 FEELING-GUILTY-ABOUT-NOT-FEELING-GUILTY

When you feel guilty about finally releasing manufactured guilt

YOU ARE BEGINNING TO UNDERSTAND the nuts and bolts of manufactured guilt, and the cumbersome furry blue Guilt Monster is finally releasing you from its relentless grip. You are utilizing the information you have thus far acquired from *Guilt Trip Detox* and are having major success. You're feeling empowered, strong, vibrant, and free, and then suddenly, out of nowhere, the Guilt Monster decides to do an encore and smashes through your protective shield of boundaries for a surprise visit.

Although you thought you were well on your way to outsmarting the Guilt Monster for eternity, its cunning nature manages to find a vulnerable sweet spot and puts you under its spell once again. Whammo, now you are **feeling-guilty-about-not-feeling-guilty**, which, when you think about it, is absurd. This last-ditch effort by the Guilt Monster often happens when you miss the old familiar rhythm of your guilt-infused thinking process. This mindset is similar to parting ways with a toxic friend you've known for years: although you are aware this person is a bad influence, somehow you still miss the *familiarity* of the old days.

Feeling-guilty-about-not-feeling-guilty is simply misread comfort. As you become more proficient at annihilating the negativity of manufactured guilt, you may experience the occasional guilty flashback about absolutely nothing. When you detox from anything, you are de-programming how you reacted in the past. It is a work in progress that you must be conscious of. Be on the lookout for any *guilt triggers*, and be ready to defend yourself if and when they arise. Continue giving the Guilt Monster the heave-ho until it realizes you mean business and its presence in your mind is no longer welcome! The more you reinforce this behavior, the more the Guilt Monster will realize you have become wise to its manipulative *guilt games* and will no longer have power over you.

Feeling-guilty-about-not-feeling-guilty is your final attempt at revisiting your old comfort zone while your new guilt-free hardware is being installed. This is another *aha* moment! You must be aware not only of the dictates of your conscious mind, which are in your focal awareness, but also of stored background messaging from your subconscious mind. Your subconscious holds stored information from your past that has the ability to creep into your present thoughts at will. It can easily influence you at any time if you let it run wild and do not question it. Do not allow the sludge of past messaging to resurface and pollute your progress. Dismiss negative thoughts of manufactured guilt immediately as they are no longer welcome to reside rent-free in your mind.

Get comfortable with your new and improved programming of living *guilt-free* and of questioning the last remnants of guilt in an expeditious manner. Perpetually acknowledge and dissolve guilty thoughts in order to stay on track!

My first experience of **feeling-guilty-about-not-feeling-guilty** occurred when I told a *guilt taskmaster* that I was unavailable to do anything for him for three days because I would be out of town. Although it was a white lie, I did this to avoid confrontation, respect my boundaries, and get some much-needed rest. Lo and behold, I had created a *staycation* for myself. I lived in my pajamas, watched movies, and took relaxing bubble baths. Knowing I had liberated myself from any obligation to this particular person, or anyone else for that matter, I had a feeling of true freedom I had not felt in a long time. Did I feel guilty? *No*, I felt empowered because I was respecting my needs by taking some much-needed time to recharge. In the past I would have felt crazy amounts of guilt doing such a thing because I had made myself unavailable and felt selfish. However, I now realize I am simply respecting my boundaries, and not harming anyone in the process, so why feel guilty?

Feeling healed and liberated, I was at the peak of my guilt-free euphoria when out of the blue, I felt a twinge of guilt about not sensing any guilt at all. Had I turned into a detached, unfeeling subhuman because I no longer felt even a remnant of guilt? I was now questioning my newfound piece of mind. I became temporarily overwhelmed by my ease of spirit and wanted to bring my unaccustomed euphoria down a few notches. Thankfully, I caught myself regressing to my old guilty comfort zone and quickly jettisoned the bothersome Guilt Monster out of my thoughts into oblivion.

Feeling guilty about not feeling guilty is the Guilt Monster's final attempt to control you. More and more, through the passing of time, you will grow to understand the deviousness and intricacies of the Guilt Monster as your awareness of its manipulative agenda expands. There is no rational reason to feel guilty about adhering to your boundaries and respecting yourself. Your guilt trips are now a thing of the past, and you will no longer feel like an unworthy pawn on the Guilt Monster's chessboard of shame and blame. Checkmate!

23 FOOD GUILT

*When you feel guilty about
your association with food*

WHY DO YOU FEEL UNWORTHY of enjoying a confluence of flavors that, when placed so tenderly in your mouth, brings you to a heightened level of delight? Generally, you block this euphoria even before the fork hits your mouth with a negative Post-it that has been Gorilla-Glued to your taste buds by none other than the Guilt Monster. Somehow, you've made yourself believe that what you eat is a moral issue, either right or wrong, good or bad. You blame yourself for every morsel you ingest, and where there's blame, guilt usually follows. Next thing you know, you start associating food with guilt.

When I was a flight attendant I would sit at airports, shoveling food in my mouth, as I awaited my next flight. I often wondered, *Did I really need that coffee and cookie, or am I eating out of sheer boredom, anxiety, and exhaustion?* I found myself constantly questioning the necessity of everything I ate, and more and more, **food guilt** was at the forefront of my thoughts. Eating versus not eating, eating versus dieting, eating versus shopping, reading, exercising, or whatever. To eat or not to eat? Once I decide *when* to eat, I must figure out *what* I should eat: white or whole wheat, organic, nondairy, gluten-free, low fat, and the list goes on.

There have been a great many food statistics and fad diets that change with the seasons. Years later, however, you hear that some of those statistics were wrong, and some of those diets were not healthy after all. Because of such findings, I yell from the rooftops for all to hear, *"Moderation!"* If your body craves something once in a while, there is usually a good reason for it. Most likely your body requires it or, heck, just wants it. Our brains are wired that way; therefore, it's not a sin to satisfy an occasional craving and enjoy a *foodie moment* guilt-free.

Why, then, do we look at eating as a moral failing that requires punishment when eating food is a necessity of life? Instead of looking at food through a lens of blame and guilt, we should be thankful and bless our food for sustaining our very existence. I believe that eating in a state of positivity leaves you feeling more satisfied and therefore not requiring extra food. If, however, you suffer from an emotional void in your psyche, which many of us do from time to time, food will NEVER fill that void and is NOT the answer to feeling whole. A counselor is the best choice in helping you overcome feelings of loneliness, depression, and low self-esteem. Getting to the root of your anxiety, sadness, hurt or unworthiness, and learning to love yourself and your life, is the answer; not food! I recommend doing your research regarding your emotional health and making it a priority to figure out what is actually driving you to eat. In the meantime, take your time and focus when eating and savor every bite in a relaxed state of mind. Be grateful for the food's sustenance instead of receiving a lashing with every bite from the Guilt Monster. Having contempt toward food is counterintuitive and creates a negative correlation; it's a dagger that pierces the heart of your healthy relationship with food.

It seems that most everyone is on a diet these days, and yet there are few long-term success stories. While most people are trying to lose weight, they are not *enjoying* anything they put in their mouths because the Guilt Monster is constantly staring at their muffin tops. Not only that, but when they finally do decide to eat, they are so busy counting calories, carbs, sodium, fat, and so on, it's a wonder there is any room left in their overwhelmed brains to process the magnificent flavor of the food.

Eating food, especially food you crave, can send your taste buds and endorphins into overdrive. Therefore, allow yourself occasional mouthfuls of soul-satisfying sustenance and fully enjoy the bliss it offers instead of instantaneously dousing your euphoria with **food guilt**. If your thoughts immediately turn negative because you have eaten from your "forbidden food" category, then you have just sucked the bliss out of your foodie moment. You look upon yourself as a failure due to your lack of willpower. Your mind then categorizes willpower as weak or strong, and because you see yourself as weak, you decide you are blameworthy and proceed to punish yourself with guilt. Once you're in the bowels of guilt, you continue eating more because you want to punish yourself for being such a failure. It's a vicious circle of negative thought that makes you angry with yourself and ruins your healthy relationship with food.

There is, however, no reason to attach punishment to a temporary setback. Setbacks are normal when changing past programming. You should EXPECT a setback, not regret it. Enforcing your food rules most of the time and allowing for an occasional reward for a job well done keeps the scales of your eating program balanced. Offering a bite of kindness to yourself here and there will translate into more success long term. Knowing you can look forward to certain foods once a week that you've eliminated from your daily regimen helps you stay on track because it gives you something to look forward to. Oftentimes, if you abstain from certain *fun* foods for long periods of time, and you aren't pleased with your weight loss results, you may lash out and binge eat on the *forbidden fruit* as a form of self-punishment. Please do not scold yourself and feel like a *loser* when you fall off your dietary wagon! Self-deprication only deflates your psyche and weakens your resolve to achieve your goals.

Instead of breaking bread with the Guilt Monster when you indulge in a meal or snack, make responsible food choices, and take time to relax and enjoy the meal without judging yourself with each and every chew. Speaking of chewing, every bite (twenty chews per bite helps slow down your eating speed, approximately 20 minutes for food to reach your stomach and feel full) should be savored. Create a positive environment when eating—light candles, put on soothing music, focus on your food and be thankful. If you are standing, walking, or talking on the phone and not giving your undivided attention to what you are eating, your brain is not focused on the bounty of flavors tickling your taste buds; therefore, it will not feel satisfied and you will be tricked into wanting and eating more. Also, focusing with laser beam precision on foods that are forbidden makes you think about them all the more. The more you think about them, the more they are at the forefront of your thoughts and the more you want them. Your brain is now on a mission to locate them. Thoughts are powerful, so be vigilant at all times about where your focus lies. YOU have the power to change your thoughts, so do so for your greater good. In order to help maintain your goals, grant yourself kindness, patience, and understanding while you change your thought patterns regarding food.

Food *choices* are important, not only regarding your weight, but also for your overall health. Make an effort to eat "clean"—organic foods without preservatives, sprays, and flavor-enhancing chemicals and dyes. When you eat at a restaurant, order a meal with nutrients, not a meal that has a lot of carbs, fillers, sodium, sugars, and sauces. Do a little research to find restaurants that offer healthy choices. Also, tell your server that you do not want additional MSG or sodium and that you would like all sauces served on the side.

If, however, your doctor puts you on a specific diet necessary for the maintenance of your health, it is wise to be as strict as possible in order to avoid medical mayhem.

There are plenty of foods to choose from out there, so do your best to make wise choices. In order to help you with this task, become more knowledgeable about food options through reading and the advice of your doctor. Knowledge is power; just don't clobber yourself if you indulge in an apple cobbler once in a while. For your next meal, make sure to banish the Guilt Monster from your table of plenty, or it will continue to force-feed you a steady diet of blame and shame with its jaw-wrenching oversized cutlery. Bon appétit!

24 GIFT-GIVING GUILT

*When you feel guilty about
buying a gift within budget*

THE ANXIETY AND GUILT SWIRLING around gift-giving can be all-consuming. How much should you spend? What do you purchase? Will the person like it? Gift giving is another scenario that has the potential for the Guilt Monster to have its way with you because it senses your vulnerability. It knows you want to express how much someone means to you by the gift you choose, but can you make this a fait accompli without overthinking it and blowing your budget?

If your colleagues decide to buy a gift for your boss's birthday and someone suggests you donate sixty dollars to the gift pool, it is up to you to decide if that amount is reasonable or excessive. One thing I've come to realize is that some people don't understand the value of another's dollar. We all have a budget to answer to, and sixty dollars may be out of your financial comfort zone. If this is the case, you must speak your mind without feeling **gift-giving guilt**. You, and you alone, are accountable for maintaining your budget in order to meet financial obligations. You must feel free to express the dollar amount you are comfortable giving. Your only concern, no matter what your collegues feel, is being responsible for living within your financial boundaries. Don't allow yourself to fall under the spell of shame or embarrassment arising from peer pressure when it comes to gift-giving—or anything else for that matter.

You may also experience a form of **gift-giving guilt** when hosting a dinner party or celebration. You want to please your guests; however, it's wise to choose gifts, food, and wines that match your financial resources. One must live within one's means, and if the Guilt Monster is your party planner, it will have the last laugh when you receive your outrageous bill as it sucks back yet another bottle of your Dom Pérignon.

Also, if you have a rich girlfriend or a financially comfortable boyfriend who loves to spoil you, that's great! Keep it coming; you deserve it! However, when it comes time to reciprocate, don't feel you have to keep pace with him or her and dig yourself into a financial hellhole. You can, of course, buy your partner something meaningful; just make sure your budget isn't being annihilated. If you cannot afford an expensive gift, a homemade dinner or handmade item will always be appreciated. Try not to obsess about gift giving or feel obligated to buy a gift that will take months to pay off, causing undue anxiety from financial despair.

I have been dating a man for a few years, and as time progresses, I find he's becoming more and more generous. There came a point at which I felt guilty about accepting his abundance of gifts as I was unable to respond in kind. With Christmas fast approaching and not knowing what to buy the man who had it all, I stumbled across the best gift ever. I was waiting in line at a novelty store, and the person behind me kept giggling. Finally, I asked her what was so funny. She looked up at me with a wide grin and said she had found the perfect gift for her boss. It was a Donald Trump doll (*The Apprentice*, pre-presidency) that came complete with twenty-four phrases that came to life when you pulled the cord on its back. Of course, it included the famous phrase "You're fired!" This doll was the perfect gift for my guy as well, I thought, because he is an executive at a large company. Cost of the doll: $9.99. *Sold!* I bought him a few other presents and came in on budget. Needless to say, my beau said it was the best Christmas gift he had received. All the "suits" in his office were fighting over the doll in the boardroom. How ironic is that? Powerful men and women grappling over a ten-dollar talking doll. Obviously, my mission was successfully accomplished, within budget, and without guilt. I'm not saying you will always be fortunate enough to find the perfect gift that lands in your price range, but with a little ingenuity, you have the power to create or purchase one without breaking the bank. Think before you buy, live within your means, and eject the wayward Guilt Monster from your sensibly filled shopping cart.

25 HAVING-IT-ALL GUILT

When you feel guilty about your good fortune

IF YOU WONDER HOW YOU came to be so fortunate to be born with a gold, silver, or platinum spoon in your smiling mouth, you may see the Guilt Monster tiptoeing around every corner, trying to snatch it away. I am one of those people. I consider myself one of the lucky ones. I was born with all my fingers, toes, and mental faculties. I come from a good home, and I never wanted for any of life's necessities. That sounds like a pretty good package, right? Life should be breezy. However, at times I feel **having-it-all guilt** because I am aware that others struggle in life's daily pursuit for a variety of reasons. Some have physical or mental disabilities, financial troubles, live in the street or war zones, or no longer have family to rely on—and the list goes on. I was particularly affected by **having-it-all guilt** because my brother has autism. He works very hard every day to complete simple tasks and communicate his thoughts, while I am able to do both, and so much more, with ease.

One particular question I continue to ask myself is *Why was I born so lucky while my brother got shortchanged?* Because of my self-imposed guilt, I have always felt I had to do everything within my power to enhance my brother's life, even though he was not always interested in living my kind of lifestyle. He prefers his days to run at a slower, more peaceful pace because he processes what he sees with more sensitivity and awareness than most. Too much stimulation is often overwhelming and exhausting to him.

In the past when I hit the dance floor, the Guilt Monster would be dancing beside me, holding up a picture of my brother as a reminder of what he was missing. I would then feel sorry for him and fall under the spell of **having-it-all guilt**. I now realize that the Guilt Monster has no right to taint my joy, because we all have different destinies, lessons, and journeys in life, my brother included. We must learn to live in our own reality, whatever that may be. There is no need to feel guilty about the gifts you possess. You were granted them for a reason, to fulfill the cycle of your destiny. It is not your responsibility to figure out all the *whys* on this planet. Simply live your life to the best of your ability with the gifts you've been granted, minus **having-it-all** guilt. Enjoy your pot of gold and utilize it to the fullest to support your journey and the journeys of others. If you feel a need to share your good fortune in order to jumpstart the release of your manufactured guilt, then giving back to those less fortunate is always appreciated.

Opportunities to pay it forward are all around you, so feel grateful you have the physical, mental, and financial means to provide, instead of putting a negative spin on your good fortune and feeling guilty. Giving to those less fortunate will create balance, make you feel worthy of your good fortune (although it is unnecessary), and add more connectivity to humanity's plight.

I have come to understand that I have absolutely no reason to feel dis-ease because I was born luckier than some. Perception is relative. How I feel about myself is relative to how I process my thoughts. I have learned it is not necessary to feel guilty and ashamed for the gift of having-it-all.

When you allow the Guilt Monster free entry into your thoughts, his negativity is never conducive to your happiness. Instead, flip your manufactured guilt into a positive. Live your life brimming with joy, which in turn elevates your spiritual vibration and exponentially transfers love to those around you. We are not in a position to control much of life's adversity, but we can control how we think and feel about it. Thinking in positives vs. guilty negatives is conducive to the betterment of everyone and is the recommended way to live.

If you've been granted good fortune, enjoy it and use it wisely. You were meant to be an inspiration and an aid to others, instead of a guilty withering soul who feels unworthy of all you possess. Live each day with a smile on your face and a spring in your step, appreciating your gifts. You are a powerful beam of light capable of creating brilliant possibilities for yourself and others. Therefore, protect your vibrant inner voltage of having-it-all from the energy depleting venom of the Guilt Monster.

26 HOLDING PATTERN GUILT

When you feel guilty about temporarily distancing yourself from someone

DO YOU HAVE A PERSON in your life who is needy, self-absorbed, obsessive, negative or who just enjoys yakking about the same old issues over and over again? Somehow you have become this person's daily life support and psychologist, and it is draining the you-know-what out of you. You like to banter with this person occasionally, but daily contact has become debilitating. Calls and visits from this person are not actual cries for help; you are simply the chosen recipient of their self-imposed drama. Hearing the same woe-is-me stories cascading from their loose lips has become toxic to you. Although you have offered the person sound advice many times, it falls on deaf ears. You come to the conclusion that the only way to preserve your sanity is to create some distance from the situation and put the person in question in a *holding pattern*.

Initially, upon realizing you had to keep a certain individual at arm's length for your own mental health, you felt the onslaught of **holding pattern guilt** as the

Guilt Monster came running towards you, guns ablazing. He or she is special to you, but the amount of time and energy spent on them as of late is consuming. After endless conversations, where all you feel you are doing is listening, you become anxious and exhausted. You know you can no longer continue down this emotionally depleting path. It is wise to reevaluate your *time boundaries* in order to avoid becoming more stressed.

If someone is diluting your energy with their perpetual drama, it's time to alert air traffic control and put your time spent with this individual in a holding pattern.

Initially, communicate to the person in question that you have given all the advice you can give regarding their issues, and have nothing further to add. If that doesn't resonate with the person, then it is wise to move forward with another line of defense. Make him or her aware that you have become very busy and are unable to have lengthy conversations. If the individual isn't adhering to your requests, then you may have to start cutting the conversations short, not answering every call, or not answering *any* calls for a period of time.

Waiting in trepidation for certain energy-depleting people to unexpectedly ring the doorbell or repeatedly phone you is not a great way to start your day. You may begin to feel on edge or trapped in your own home or office, wondering if the person is close to paying you another soul-draining visit. You have been cornered one too many times by Ms. or Mr. Drama Extraordinaire. Evasive action is necessary to protect your boundaries, or else you are going to burn off more of your precious brain cells. The Guilt Monster's thunderous voice blares, "How can you treat others so poorly by not taking their calls and avoiding them? How selfish of you!" Instead of listening to its rhetoric and allowing yourself to be brainwashed and feel **holding pattern guilt**, start by listening to your own inner voice of reason and make certain your energy and *privacy boundaries* are being honored.

Your decision to create temporary distance from someone is a necessary action to restore peace of mind. As much as it is a difficult decision—you do not want to alienate or upset anyone—you desperately need to regain your tranquility. Do not allow the Guilt Monster to slime you with **holding pattern guilt** as you untangle yourself from the web of angst felt every time your cell or doorbell rings. *Ding-dong! Ding-dong! Ding-dong!*

Sometimes a little distance allows people the necessary time to think about their issues instead of being reactionary and venting about them haphazardly to anyone within earshot. Reflection vs. reaction. People that *reflect* focus on dealing with their problems internally instead of habitually deflecting them onto others. Reactionary people tend to vent their emotions with little or no forethought to anyone within strike range.

Sometimes, however, nothing is gained from your temporary reprieve from someone you have in a holding pattern. The person may not *get it*. If this is the case, you may have to extend the holding pattern for a longer period of time or forever—whatever your good counsel suggests. If they have a problem that is constantly repeated, perhaps suggest professional help to aid in its resolution.

It is important to be particular with those whom you spend quality time They may feel comfortable unleashing their innermost thoughts to you. However, if you've offered them repeated advice and there is no change in their scenario, you may have to bring the subject matter to a grinding halt. They may then realize they are talking in circles and try to find other solutions to deal with their problems. In any event, it is up to you to respect and protect your privacy and time boundaries. As for the Guilt Monster constantly badgering you about your selfishness after putting someone in a *holding pattern*, the blue beast needs to mind its own business and be immediately unfriended, blocked, and deleted from your thoughts.

27 HOLIDAY GUILT

When you feel guilty for not celebrating noteworthy days

THERE ARE MANY HOLIDAYS OR special calendar days that people around the world celebrate. Some of these days people pay homage to are religiously motivated, and others are not. Nonetheless, they are considered special days that people identify with. Some examples are Christmas, Passover, Ramadan, Diwali, Indigenous People's Day, Thanksgiving, Easter, Cinco de Mayo, Bastille Day, Mardi Gras, New Year's Eve, Saint Patrick's Day, Valentine's Day, Veterans Day, Martin Luther King Jr. Day, Mother's Day, Father's Day, Halloween, and Chinese New Year. Birthdays and anniversaries, although not holidays, can also be included under the umbrella of *holiday guilt*.

Everyone has their own set of standards when it comes to how they celebrate their chosen holidays. When you forget or haven't fulfilled your supposed obligation on these special days, you have a tendency to feel the Guilt Monster painting you into a dark corner of shame. You sense the judgmental eyes of others upon you because of your lack of involvement. If you completely forget a special holiday, **holiday guilt** can be overwhelming in relation to how severely you may have upset someone. Others expected you to acknowledge the holiday with fanfare, and because you did not participate or did not show enough exuberance, you now reside in their *holiday doghouse*. You feel the heavy reverberations of their dismay. "Shame on you for forgetting this important holiday! Shame on you for not buying a gift! Shame on you for not showing up to our special dinner!" Now, instead of eating the celebratory meal, you are eating the bitter leftover scraps of **holiday guilt.**

Everyone has their own idea how best to entertain during a holiday, and everyone has their own set of limitations, so don't compare yourself to others and feel guilty because you do not share the same enthusiasm or beliefs. Always refer back to your unique set of boundaries. Perhaps you are inundated with responsibilities and lack the necessary time to celebrate, or maybe you're too tired from work or weak from an illness. Perhaps you are financially unable to accommodate a holiday feast or gifts, or maybe you simply aren't interested at all or forgot the holiday altogether. Your holiday, or lack thereof, unfolded the way it did for a reason and others should respect that. Run spryly in the opposite direction when someone throws you a Molotov shame-on-you cocktail. No one has the right to judge you, so do not allow anyone the power to poison your thoughts and emotions.

One of my holiday guilt stories takes place before Christmas and revolves around my Christmas tree. I had been feeling more tired than usual and was in no mood to dig out the tree and all the trimmings from the bowels of my basement, haul it all up a flight of stairs, untangle the lights, hang up the decorations, and then vacuum all the pine needles and tinsel strewn on the carpet. For this particular year, I decided the Nativity scene was a sufficient representation of Christmas. After all, Christmas is about celebrating the birth of Jesus and not about a pine tree. My daughters were older at the time, and when asked if it made a difference whether we graced our house with a Christmas tree, they were indifferent. I told them if they were so inclined, *they* could decorate the tree minus my participation. They declined.

As Christmas approached, I felt sporadic **holiday guilt** every time my friends mentioned how beautiful their Christmas trees looked, knowing I had *not* gone the distance to erect one of these holiday symbols myself. When my friends found out I was *tree-less*, they were aghast and thought I'd gone mad! The Guilt Monster was working its magic on me, holding my Christmas tree in one paw and whirling a lasoo of multicolored lights over its head with the other, awaiting my capture. I thought, *Am I a bad mom? Am I lazy? Am I becoming a nonbeliever?* Although I knew none of that was true, I felt guilty nonetheless because I was led to believe I had broken an unwritten holiday rule.

As it turned out, there was absolutely nothing to feel guilty about. I was just creating manufactured guilt because I was allowing others to blur my decisions and boundaries. Was I a lesser person for not displaying a tree? Absolutely not! It was a very merry Christmas, minus the added work, back pain, and stress of a tree setup. The next year I had more time and energy on my hands and enjoyed the pleasantries of decorating a Christmas tree, albeit a smaller one, which was a less arduous task. Did I do so because of **holiday guilt**, you ask? Absolutely not! I decorated the baby tree because it was easier to put together and I had missed the soothing atmosphere of the colorful lights.

Thanksgiving celebrations delivered another dose of holiday guilt to be reckoned with. One year I decided I was not going to stuff and cook yet another turkey. I just didn't want to go there, up to my elbow in the cavity of an ice-cold fowl and pulling out all the parts that no one eats anyway. The last thing I wanted to be in charge of was hosting a full Thanksgiving dinner with all the trimmings. I informed my family that we were going to order Chinese food for Thanksgiving dinner instead. Upon hearing the news of this break in tradition, my daughters were absolutely horrified. "We need to have a turkey! It won't be the same without one!" they exclaimed. I immediately felt the chi being sucked right out of me by the Guilt Monster's syringe of shame because I was disappointing my family and not living up to our previous Thanksgiving standards. I told my daughters that if they wanted a turkey dinner that badly, they would have to participate in its preparation because I was tired, and "the turkey does not magically appear ready-cooked on your plate." I was thrilled that my daughters were happy to oblige. We had fun preparing the feast together, instead of me preparing it alone and bitchin' in the kitchen. They got their stuffed turkey, and I got the help I needed. Let it be known that in future years, we had many *turkey-less* Thanksgiving dinners, and the only thing that did get stuffed was the Guilt Monster.

I am writing about holidays that I am familiar with, but no matter which special days you celebrate, guilt is not necessary if your participation, or lack thereof, is not in alignment with the expectations of others. Set boundaries for yourself in advance regarding how you wish to modify your celebration. Communicate your desires with those involved, and try to strike a happy holiday medium. May your holidays hold a special place in your heart, no matter when, how, or if you celebrate them, and may your ultimate decision fill you with jubilation instead of the Guilt Monster's tribulation.

28 HONESTY GUILT

When you feel guilty for telling someone the truth

ANOTHER RED-HOT GUILT TOPIC IS honesty guilt. When you are honest with someone because he or she asked for your upfront opinion, you may not always be received with open arms. Sometimes telling the truth hurts the recipient, especially if your honest answer is not what the other person was expecting to hear. You had no intent to hurt anyone; you were only delivering a straightforward answer, as asked, which you thought would help them see the forest for the trees.

My friend Abigail was upset about her boyfriend for a long period of time, and she wanted to know my straightforward opinion on the matter. She had fretted over the same issue for months in many of our conversations, and I had remained silent about my observations so as not to upset her. Eventually I came to the conclusion that in order to help and hopefully relieve her perpetual misery, I would not sugarcoat my opinion any longer. I suggested that, when talking about issues with her boyfriend, she should try using a calmer tone and perhaps not be so demanding. Well, after the most grueling five-second pregnant pause ever experienced by humankind, she said, "How dare you insinuate that I'm to blame!" Not only did I get lambasted by my friend, but I was quickly shown the door. I had been emotionally pulverized for sharing my honest opinion as asked. At that moment, the Guilt Monster made its grand entrance in all its colorful regalia, upstaging my honesty and yelling from the rooftops that I was cold and unfeeling and should have taken my friend's side no matter what!

I felt horrible about upsetting my friend and somehow decided I deserved to be punished for hurting her feelings. The Guilt Monster expeditiously presented my **honesty guilt** to me on its best china. It's ludicrous that I wanted to punish myself with guilt for being honest, but such is the nature of the beast, until you learn to understand guilt and stop it from further manipulating you.

For a while I had a knot in my stomach the size of Manhattan from the *guilties*, but after further thought, I realized my honesty was something I would not forfeit. I adored my friend and felt she needed to hear the truth in order to gain perspective. At the very least it would offer food for thought. At the risk of upsetting her, I considered it my duty to be completely honest.

Was this disagreement the final curtain call for our long friendship? As it turned out, our friendship got back on track after the sting of reality subsided and my friend realized that what I had said was helpful. In this case, the only reason one should feel guilty is for *not* being honest, especially when asked. As I see it, if you are not living in truth, you are living a lie. Lies aren't real, so in essence you are not *truly* living and evolving.

Honesty, although at times painful to hear, enlightens and offers perspective. Honesty is always the best policy. Never allow the Guilt Monster the power to derail the delivery of your honest opinion to another.

29 INSTITUTION GUILT

When you feel guilty about your association with an institution

I'M SURE YOU'VE HEARD THE phrase "guilt by association." You may feel this way when you are associated with an institution that has been involved in actions you are not proud of or no longer believe in. Institutions are organizations created for religious, professional, educational, or social purposes. Institutions are built on pillars of rules and regulations and govern the behavior of a particular community.

When the institution you are affiliated with has committed a wrongdoing, you have the potential to feel a transference of their guilt falling heavily on your shoulders. Let's explore the inner workings of the Vatican as an example. The Vatican is an institution built on trust, faith, hope, love, and the teachings of Jesus Christ. When it became crystal clear that priests were molesting children entrusted to their care, it was an abomination of the very beliefs Catholics stand for. Some parishioners experienced **institution guilt** because of their proximity with the institution. In order to absolve it, they had either quit attending church or began to voice their outrage loudly and relentlessly in the hopes of restoring justice.

Years later, society demanded a global apology from the Vatican, which eventually took place. Pope John Paul II decided that for the year 2000, the Jubilee year, the church couldn't "cross the threshold of the new millennium" without asking forgiveness for its past shortcomings. Although the Vatican took an initial step to acknowledge the rampant child abuse in the Catholic Church, the perpetrators were never brought to justice, and the church's walk of shame continued.

The Vatican has since taken affirmative action and created additional steps to streamline complaints and punish predators, as well as anyone who chooses to conceal a predator's history, by forever relieving them of their duties. The new rules are being implemented thanks to ongoing collective screams from society demanding that predators pay for their misdeeds instead of being sheltered within the walls of the church.

Although you may be associated with institutions that are guilty of crimes, you should never allow the Guilt Monster to transfer the blame onto you unless you were personally responsible or aware in advance of the injustice and remained silent. In good conscience, you should feel an obligation to voice your concerns about any institution's acts of unlawfulness to the necessary authorities in a timely manner.

Another example of **institution guilt** revolves around unscrupulous actions of governments. Germany's government during the late thirties and early forties when Adolf Hitler was in power is a prime example. Although Hitler was supposed to represent the people of Germany, he manipulated and threatened them instead. He had no problem ordering the executions of millions of Jews and anyone else who posed a threat to his ideology, including his own people. Although German citizens participated in the war—most feared for their lives if they didn't—does that mean if you are of German descent, you should feel guilty? Of course not!

Unfortunately, some German citizens continue to suffer from **institution guilt** because of the heinous crimes of their past government. The treachery caused by an institution you are affiliated with is not reason enough for you to become bedfellows with the Guilt Monster. If you feel remorse about your affiliation, own it, meditate on it, learn from it, and release it. Wearing the yoke of lingering guilt is unnecessary and debilitating to your self-worth and joy.

Unfortunately, the tyranny of some governments will not end anytime soon, but as a whole, we must always believe in freedom and justice and learn from our past errors. In our world, genocide, abuse of women and children, and cruelty in general abounds. Many of these barbaric acts are fueled by institutional rhetoric. Witnessing these atrocities on television often makes me feel like I'm being squeezed between Guilt Monster bookends on an all too short ledge. I feel guilty for not doing something to stop the madness, but I don't know where to start. After further thought, I realized that it is not guilt I feel, but an inner awakening regarding how I may make contributions toward solving global injustices.

I have since signed petitions for groups on the internet that represent those less fortunate. These groups work on the behalf of aggrieved people to help them regain peace, justice, dignity, and human rights. The more voices involved, the louder the thunder, and the greater the chance for accountability and reform to prevail. We must all find the courage to speak out in order to maintain the accountability of our institutions. Do not allow **institution guilt** to tarnish your affiliation with an organization that has been marred by a few wayward souls. If we collectively stand up for justice and the betterment of our institutions, we'll stand down from their wrongdoing and cease wearing the Guilt Monster's heavy robe of shame.

30 INTUITION GUILT

*When you feel guilty about
listening to your instincts*

WHEN YOU HAVE A GUT feeling or inner sense about something, it is usually your intuition trying to guide you. As it turns out, this little voice within happens to know a heck of a lot about what is best for YOU! This beneficial guidance system can make you feel uncomfortable, because it delivers advice you didn't necessarily ask for, and comes from a source you are unable to trace. You second-guess the recommendations of your intuition because it doesn't always make sense to you at the time. Down the road, however, you come to realize that if you had listened to its advice, it would have spared you some grief.

There are times you may feel **intuition guilt** because your instincts are in complete opposition of others. In order to appease others' wishes and avoid confrontation, you discount the self-protective advice from your intuition and try to meet others halfway, or give in completely, and meet them all the way. When guilt starts toying with your intuition's counsel and you dismiss its advice, you usually find yourself bobbing in a sea of regrets.

Here is a story about a young woman who ignored her intuition twice in one day. She decided to go shopping for a living room suite and brought her mom along for the ride, even though her intuition warned her not to bring her mom. She wanted to include her mom because she thought it would be a positive bonding experience since their relationship was not particularly warm and fuzzy. As it turned out, discounting her intuition and having her mom join her, ended up causing a great deal of disappointment. The two of them had opposite tastes in many areas, including furniture. The young woman loved modern furniture, whereas her mom preferred traditional. In the hopes of having a better relationship with her mom, the daughter decided to buy the living room suite her mom fancied instead of listening to the advice of her intuition. Now, every time she enters her living room, the couch blares "Mama's old school couch" with the Guilt Monster fully outstretched on it as she recoils at the sight of them both.

The young woman has tried with all her might to find something to like about the living room suite, but it just isn't her style and never will be. Had she not taken her mom shopping, as her intuition warned her not to, and bought the couch her intuition approved of, she would be enjoying her new purchase instead of dreading the daily sight of it. Eventually, she got rid of the couch, as she could no longer stand looking at it, and found the courage to overstep her mom's opinion and her guilt and bought a couch she loves. Now she enjoys relaxing on it and watching a movie, minus the sprawling Guilt Monster taking over her thoughts and ruining her night.

I also have a personal story about intuition guilt. One evening while getting ready to go to a Christmas party, my intuition screamed at me to stay home. I fought the feeling relentlessly, asking why I shouldn't attend. I promised my friend I'd be there, but somehow it didn't feel right to go. In order to please my friend and acquiesce to her wishes, I turned a blind eye to my intuition and went to the party nonetheless. I left the soiree early as I continued to feel uneasy all night and thought it best to get home sooner rather than later. I drove home very slowly, on the lookout for what my intuition was trying to warn me about earlier. I arrived home safely, parked the car in the garage, and gasped a sigh of relief. Phew, home safe and sound. Seeing it was such a beautiful night, I decided to stay outside a little longer to get some air. I then made the decision to check the mailbox at my front door. It was winter, so I was extra cautious and looked for ice on the front step. The coast was clear, no ice anywhere. I then placed my focus on the mailbox and proceeded to put my right foot on the front step to take a peek inside. As I'd had my walkway raised a few months prior, and because I use the front door very infrequently, muscle memory took over and I put my foot down where the step used to be for the last thirty years, three inches higher. My right foot was actually in the air when I sprang up with my left foot. I was weightless for a second, and then all hell broke loose as I came crashing down on the concrete with my full body weight. I blacked out, and when I awoke, I was sitting in the opposite direction with all three bones in my ankle broken; my left foot was lifeless and sitting flat against the concrete. I let out two bloodcurdling screams. Luckily, the neighbor's son was in his car talking to his girlfriend on his cell phone, heard my screams, came to my aid and called an ambulance. The point of the story is, had I listened to my intuition and not allowed guilt to intervene with my internal guidance system, I would not have broken my ankle and caused myself, and those who later took care of me, an immense inconvenience.

Never second-guess your sixth sense in an attempt to please others. Each person has different tastes, paths, opinions, and destinies. Your intuition offers information that is strictly scripted for YOU! Jump off the **intuition guilt** carousel (yes, even while it's spinning), and be true to your inner wisdom. Pleasing others in order to avoid guilt, at your intuition's expense, will leave you disappointed or worse. When you respect your intuition, you are respecting yourself. When you have faith in your intuition, life will unfold with greater ease following a blueprint designed specifically for you. Your intuition will guide and protect you, and in turn, melt the Guilt Monster into a puddle of powerless blue goo.

31 | JOB RESPONSIBILITY GUILT

*When you feel guilty about
job responsibilities infringing
on your free time*

"GET THE FINAL DRAFT ON my desk ASAP!"

"I need this proofread before you go home tonight!"

"Have the paperwork on this new client ready first thing tomorrow morning!"

Do the demands of your job have you grinding out more hours than you signed up for and carving away at your downtime with friends and family? You want to keep the boss happy by being a conscientious employee, but when job responsibilities interfere with time shared with loved ones, your new Saks suit is in jeopardy of getting slimed by the Guilt Monster.

Lately the Guilt Monster has taken up permanent residency on your desk while it polishes its horns with your cashmere scarf, watching you tend to yet another task and missing another dinner with friends or family. You work hard to make ends meet to create a better lifestyle for those nearest and dearest, so don't feel guilty for not always being available. Life is difficult to keep in balance at the best of times; therefore, why feel guilty? Those special people in your life will have to understand that in order to enjoy the fruits of your labor, at times sacrifices must be made. Fulfilling job responsibilities is necessary to provide the basics of life as well as added extras, such as vacations, cars, and entertainment. With company cutbacks, wages not keeping pace with inflation, and working extended hours without added compensation, it becomes increasingly difficult to balance quality in the workplace with quality of life. Working long hours and missing another important dinner or event with loved ones can easily infuse you with blame and guilt as they display their disappointment yet again.

Although working for a living is a reality of life and you are aware that your **job responsibility guilt** is manufactured, you continue trying to de-slime your guilt-filled office. There are, however, several things to aid you in silencing these guilty reverberations. If, for instance, you have a job that takes you out of town, and the Guilt Monster has become your constant travel companion, then it's time to reconnect more often with family and friends. Zoom, FaceTime, and WhatsApp are a few ways to achieve this. A phone call a day keeps the Guilt Monster away. Having regular conversations with those you care about offers an opportunity for everyone to feel connected and acknowledged. It's cathartic to express one's concerns in real time before they have the opportunity to grow into an anger or anxiety projectile, wreaking havoc on anyone within strike range—in particular, you.

When time spent with family and friends is inadequate and they become displeased, it's time for some preemptive action before the Guilt Monster becomes permanently entangled in your toupee or updo. A vacation or a movie night is a great way to keep family and friend links well-oiled. You could plan to have loved ones accompany you on an occasional business trip, or perhaps take a few personal days off to bring your home life back into balance. Also, if your commute to work is taking a huge bite out of your day, consider moving closer to your place of employ, instead of walking through the door at the end of your exhausting commute to witness the Guilt Monster nestled between your kids on the couch watching movies. Whether you decide to make executive changes or not, keep the lines of communication open with those you love. Let them know you always have their best interests at heart, even though your time with them is at a premium. You are working long hours to provide for yourself and others, and if anything, your efforts should be applauded.

Staring into the Guilt Monster's purple eyes of contempt, as it peeks into your cubicle is *never* advantageous. Feeling proud of your efforts as a breadwinner is! You are fortunate to be gainfully employed with a job that provides for the necessities of life and more, so pat yourself on the back for a job well done and immediately fire the Guilt Monster from being the CEO of your thoughts.

32 LEARNING-THE-LESSON GUILT

When you feel guilty about not learning a lesson sooner

LEARNING-THE-LESSON GUILT HAS THE ABILITY to make you feel guilty twice—once for feeling like a failure for your shortcomings, and a guilt encore for not having learned the lesson sooner. Do not give the Guilt Monster permission to spin you around in a centrifuge at dizzying speeds because you haven't awarded yourself an A-plus for learning a life lesson in record time. The speed of your learning is not important as long as you are always trying your best. The Guilt Monster is not your judge and jury and has no right to hammer the gavel on your soul while you maneuver through life's many hairpin curves.

Every living soul has their own unique bucketful of lessons to learn. While working on YOUR lessons, don't compare yourself to others that already "get it" because they have different lessons to learn that you don't. No one is perfect, even if they believe they are, so refrain from browbeating yourself with **learning-the-lesson guilt**. It is unnecessary punishment that can lead to a depressed state. Instead, be thankful for the lesson that has granted you the opportunity to grow and blossom into a more aware human being.

When you have learned a lesson, especially a particularly difficult one, meditate on what created the situation in the first place, learn what you can about it, and try to avoid future occurrences. Always be patient and compassionate with yourself along the way while reflecting on and growing from your lesson.

If **learning-the-lesson guilt** continues to linger, it helps to forgive yourself for past failings or oversights, as well as asking for the forgiveness of others that your shortcomings may have affected. Your state of consciousness is always growing and expanding, so cut yourself some slack when trying to understand the causes and effects of past decisions and actions. Learning lessons is normal, and guilt is a manufactured emotion that is not conducive to learning and healing; therefore, banish it immediately from your thoughts! Always be patient with your growth and the answers will come; Rome wasn't built in a day. Start today and be thankful for the lessons that have enlightened you during your journey. Always be hopeful, and look forward to the brilliance of tomorrow utilizing your newly obtained wisdom. Whether you are a fast or slow study is not important, as long as you eventually "get it." Learning lessons is a fact of life, so go with the flow and do your best. Move forward with your newfound awareness with confidence. Continue your journey of self-discovery with patience, compassion and understanding, instead of needlessly kicking yourself with the Guilt Monster's steel-toed boots of blame.

33 LETDOWN GUILT

When you feel guilty about not living up to the expectations of others

ONE OF THE REASONS I experienced the full force of **letdown guilt** was that I did not take the advice of my parents and attend university. They strategically bought a house near a university with the intention that I attend after finishing high school. My parents also offered to pay my full tuition. As simple as it would have been to acquire more education, I didn't possess a passion to study any particular subject and did not want to waste their hard-earned money. I chose instead to put my education on hold until I decided exactly what I wanted to be when I grew up. In the meantime, I thought I'd become a flight attendant for a few years in order to see the world and think about my future. As life unfolded, I met my future husband, got married, built a house, and became pregnant with twin daughters. Game, set, match! My future took on a life of its own, and my goal of eventually attending university became a mere pipe dream. As I reflected on my parents' lofty hopes of their child attending university being forever lost, I felt inundated with **letdown guilt**.

As time passed, I realized I had no reason to feel guilty about disappointing my parents as they were thrilled about how my life had unfolded. They were pleased I had a job I enjoyed, a beautiful family, and many travel perks. They were also ecstatic at becoming the proud grandparents of twin granddaughters.

My guilt trip was a figment of my overactive imagination. What a waste of energy, feeling regret and shame arising from manufactured **letdown guilt**. The only person I actually *let down* was myself. Even if my parents had not been thrilled about my choices, I shouldn't have borne the brunt of their disappointment because life turned out differently from what they had hoped; after all, it's MY life. Allowing guilt to pump through your veins because you don't feel you've lived up to someone's expectations is harmful to your psyche. You will never be able to please everyone, even if you try, but then again, why would you want to? Everyone's destiny is unique, so do what's best for YOU.

A female friend of mine became a lawyer only to live up to the expectations of her father. She felt guilty pursuing a career in fashion because she didn't want to disappoint daddy. She begrudgingly finished law school and practiced her profession for seven grueling years to avoid the wrath of **letdown guilt**. One day she realized she could no longer tolerate her job. She detested it with every ounce of her being. She wanted to run as far away as possible from her present reality and burn all her lawbooks in the nearest incinerator. She needed a break, or else she was going to have a breakdown. She granted herself some much-needed time off to decompress and re-evaluate her life. While on sabbatical, she saw an advertisement from a film company looking for a wardrobe assistant. She decided to apply on a whim. She not only nailed the interview but was also offered the job. Start date: three weeks! She was thrilled to the moon and back about finally having a job that was in a field she was passionate about.

After years of being handcuffed to the Guilt Monster, my friend kicked it out of her office and made the life-changing decision to temporarily abandon law while she took a whirl as a wardrobe assistant for a major film company. She ended up loving her new job and lifestyle, which was brimming with more freedom, excitement, and adventure than she could have ever imagined. She was finally doing something that nourished her soul, and slowly but surely, her stress and anxiety began to diminish. Eventually, she mustered all her courage to inform her father that she was no longer a lawyer, and her new job title was "wardrobe assistant."

Her father was mortified at hearing the news, and my friend felt every pore of her body saturated in **letdown guilt**. She wrestled with the Guilt Monster for a short while, but eventually wiggled out of its hold, squishing the beast back into the dark recesses of her abandoned briefcase and clicking it shut. After a period of adjustment, her father accepted his daughter's new job title as he could see how much happier she had become. Eventually, she met her significant other at work, and they now live happily ever after with their dog Scruffy.

Ultimately, you are here to fulfill YOUR destiny, not someone else's. Figure out who you are and what makes you happy, and go after it! Be your own best friend, and be proud of your choices big and small, right or wrong. They are YOURS to own! Moreover, don't allow anyone the right to say "I told you so" if things don't turn out the way you had hoped. Life is about the journey, not perfection.

Think like Muhammad Ali: *"I am the greatest!"* I met Mr. Ali many years ago, and let me say this, he was not swayed even a millimeter by people's opinion or expectations of him. He was a man of conviction who *owned* all his decisions. There were times when he made difficult choices that were not always well received by the public, but he did what he believed was right for him and him alone! The word *guilt* was definitely not part of his vocabulary. If needed, he would easily knock out the Guilt Monster with one of his electrifying smiles that radiated awareness, determination, and unbridled self-confidence. Pow!

34 LIVING-YOUR-DREAMS GUILT

When you feel guilty for accepting opportunities to live your dreams

IN YOUR HEART YOU MAY believe that the phrase "living your dreams" is indeed only a dream. Instead of believing that your future aspirations will come to fruition, you subconsciously sabotage their eventuality, even when they come knocking at your door. You may self-sabotage for a host of reasons: you feel guilty living your dreams while others are not, you feel unworthy of such a privilege, or you feel you will be abandoning others.

My mother's story is a great example of **living-your-dreams guilt.** Mom is an amazing singer and performer. She was born with beauty, perfect pitch, powerful pipes, and a natural love for commanding a stage. I was always in awe watching her perform, as was everyone in the audience, and we became mesmerized by her beautiful voice and charismatic stage presence. When she performed, she was in her element, it was without a doubt one of her happy places. One fateful day, some professional musicians who had recorded and sold many albums worldwide heard her sing at a festival and invited her to record with them in Toronto, just a two-hour plane ride from her home. She declined the offer because she felt guilty that her family might fall apart while she was temporarily out of town. *Gong!* Wrong answer! Here is a woman who, when granted the opportunity of a lifetime to do exactly what she loved and was gifted to do, refused the offer on account of manufactured guilt. The Guilt Monster sabotaged her glorious opportunity by instilling her with fear that her family would pay the consequences if she were away temporarily. This manufactured feeling made her believe her dream was an impossibility. She could not fathom how she could simultaneously juggle raising her family and living her dreams without serious repercussions and a whole lot of guilt.

If my mother had thought it through rationally, before the Guilt Monster hid her microphone, she would have been well on her way down the yellow brick road of making her dreams come true. Perhaps she could have flown back and forth between recording sessions, arranged for a housecleaning service to help out, or taken her family with her. With a little creative thought, there is always a way to live your dreams if you believe in them strongly, work hard, and do not become fearful and guilt-ridden when the doors of opportunity open. Where there's a will, there's a way, and those with the most *will*, win!

It is highly probable my mother would have earned a living doing what she was so passionate about, instead of working at her job on an uninspiring bakery production line. The lifestyle of a performer definitely would have been more suited to her larger-than-life personality and awesome voice. It was a terrible waste of talent that otherwise would have brought joy to her many fans, her family, and most importantly, herself.

Much later in life, after reflecting on her choices, she said she would have decided differently and accepted the offer to record. Although her big chance has come and gone, she has learned to keep the Guilt Monster away from her microphone and out of her life. My mother harbors no regrets because she loves her life nonetheless. **Living-your-dreams guilt** will never get in her way again, because she learned to face her fears. Although Mom is now eighty years old, you can still catch her serenading an audience at her assisted-living home to thunderous applause.

I also have a personal story about **living-your-dreams guilt**. On a whim, I went to Los Angeles to meet up with a friend. I was twenty-two, full of adventure, and heading to the land of milk and honey. When I landed, he was at the airport waiting for me, but I was unrecognizable. My long hair was tucked inside a Gatsby-ish hat, I was not wearing makeup, and I had dark circles under my eyes. I looked a little worse for wear because I had been up for forty consecutive hours recording a music demo before my flight. My friend finally recognized me when I called out to him. He immediately informed me we were expected at a party. I told him to go without me because I was overtired and needed some sleep. He said we were both on the guest list and should at least make an appearance, so I agreed to accompany him for a short time.

After getting lost in Bel Air, we finally found the

location of the party. A voice coming from an intercom built into the side of a huge rock asked for our names. Soon, two large metal gates to the property opened. As I found out later, we were at the Playboy Mansion, and unbeknownst to me, it was Academy Awards night. The place was swirling with well-dressed celebrities, and everyone was dancing and having fun. I, on the other hand, was tired and not dressed for such a glamorous event. Later that evening, I found out my friend had shared one of my bathing suit modeling photographs with Hugh Hefner's assistant. She immediately passed it on to Mr. Hefner, and he approved it on the spot for a *Playboy* centerfold.

Although I had no premeditated desire to appear in *Playboy*, I thought it might help advance my singing career. Unfortunately, the Guilt Monster was at Mr. Hefner's party as well, and what kept going through my mind was *My mother will have my head on a platter if I go ahead with this photo shoot.* Guilt obliterated my thinking and took over the controls. Instead of being the captain of my decisions, I allowed the Guilt Monster to make my decision for me. In the end I probably wouldn't have accepted the offer even if the Guilt Monster was nowhere in sight; however, I allowed the Guilt Monster to have the last word.

I have since learned to stop such destructive behavior and now believe in the power of ME instead of allowing the Guilt Monster to be my *dream buster.*

It's difficult enough trying to accomplish your dreams, so please, please, pretty please, do not allow guilt to sabotage the wonderful opportunities you receive along life's way, many of which occur once in a lifetime. Be adventurous and get familiar with the true rhythm of your spirit. Whether you succeed or fail, you will learn a great deal about yourself and have no regrets. We only get so many chances, and then they are gone forever, so give them serious rational thought and take advantage of them as they arise. Feel the excitement pump through your veins as you take that scary leap of faith into making your dreams a reality. Outside influences may not always agree with your executive decisions, and that is their right. But it is YOUR right to fulfill your destiny. Stay true to your desires, and never allow the Guilt Monster to turn your magnificent dreams into a dreaded nightmare of regret.

35 MISTAKE/ACCIDENT GUILT

When you feel guilty about an error

WHEN YOU MAKE A *MISTAKE*, which is defined as an error in judgement, or are involved in an *accident*, which is defined as an unfortunate incident; both instances have the potential to make you feel blameworthy and deserving of a large dose of guilt. Guilt, however, is not necessary, because mistakes and accidents happen unintentionally. There is nothing premeditated about them; therefore, there is no need to dunk yourself in a vat of guilt due to your involvement in unforeseen misfortune. Unfortunately, it is *normal* for mistakes and accidents to happen.

When mistakes and accidents take place, take some time to unwind from the ensuing shock and review the event in order to learn from it and heal. Grant yourself some well-deserved compassion and try to move forward instead of being tackled to the ground and pummeled by the Guilt Monster. It is understandable that a certain amount of remorse or anger will be felt for the regrettable way a situation unfolded; however, over time it is best to release the burden and forge ahead.

Mistakes and accidents sometimes have a way of creating defining moments in your life, depending on their degree of severity, that may scar your psyche while you process the fallout of the *event*. Most times, circumstances were out of your control, and forgiving yourself and others, is the best medicine. Forgive, over and over again if necessary, in order to regain peace of mind that will allow you to move forward more effortlessly. Refrain from blaming yourself and others for the aftermath of unexpected, unfortunate circumstances out of one's control.

Your basement floods, but you forgot to pay your house insurance and now you don't have the assets to rebuild; or you sold your father's house soon after he passed away and later felt deep regret about selling the family home. These are scenarios in which you made an error in judgment, upset someone or yourself unwittingly, and now feel you must pay the consequences by feeling guilty. At times, temporary guilt can be cathartic as you process your feelings attached to the misfortune, but in the end, it must be released. You were not born in a paint-by-numbers world that is neatly laid out for you in all its perfection. Know that mistakes, miscalculations and accidents will occur for reasons unbeknownst to us. That is a fact of life, albeit not a pleasant one. Please stop wearing yourself out with anger, regret and guilt because you made an error or were in the wrong place at the wrong time.

Some mistakes and accidents are tragic, such as sliding on the ice while driving and causing a horrific car accident where someone gets hurt or dies. Mistakes and accidents come in all shapes and sizes, and there are countless variables that contribute to how a situation unfolds. Gazing into your hindsight mirror, you wonder how on earth you made such a stupid mistake or didn't see an accident coming. "Where was my head?" you ask. Actually, your head was right where it should be; you were unfortunately involved in a situation that was simply beyond your control. You now have two choices: You can continue to feel the misery of **mistake/accident guilt** or you can accept you are imperfectly human and forgive yourself of the unwanted event and move forward.

Bombarding yourself with long-term soul crushing guilt is never the winning answer! It keeps you stuck in a dark period of your past and rejects any future joy that comes your way because you feel you don't *deserve* it. When you choose to be blinded by guilt, you are unable to see the goodness and beauty that continues to surround you. Keep in mind that most accidents and mistakes are a one-off that you didn't see coming. Although you may never forget the gravity of your mistake or accident, please don't continue to persecute yourself by rewinding the tape and emotionally reliving the anger, regret and blame. Deciding to continually drag the past into your future only gives the Guilt Monster free rein to pulverize you with his mortar and pestle, then take the fine dust of your crushed happiness and toss it into the wind, lost forever. This is NOT a pretty picture, and NOT the way you want to live the rest of your days!

Try meditating daily on forgiving yourself and asking for peace of mind to lighten the load your soul is carrying. If you still find it difficult to heal, try giving back to the individuals involved or to the community associated with your mistake or accident. Try to create something positive from your misfortune if possible. This is forward moving and powerfully healing, instead of remaining stuck in your mind's prison after sentencing yourself to a lifetime of guilt. Gradually, melt away the dismal emotions of **mistake/ accident guilt** and carry on with the joy of living. Your days of persecution will soon be over when the Guilt Monster is no longer the warden of your mind.

36 PAYBACK GUILT

When you feel guilty because you are unable to reciprocate a good deed

SOMEONE IS THERE TO HELP you in your time of need, but the Guilt Monster is sucking the jubilation out of your fortuitous moment because you have no way to repay this kind act. The universe, in all its infinite power, has a way of sending you aid at your most vulnerable times. You are not expected to accomplish everything alone or to payback anyone tit for tat, dollar for dollar. Simply learn to graciously accept someone's assistance along life's way and sincerely thank the person; that is all. If you want to give the person a token of thanks, such as a bottle of wine or invite them over for dinner, that is acceptable but never necessary. If you refuse someone's help because you feel too proud, unworthy, or guilty, or because you are unable to pay the person back, it will negatively impact your life because in doing this you close yourself off to the natural flow of the world's give-and-take.

People help others because they choose to; no one is twisting their arm, holding a gun to their head, or giving them an ultimatum. If it makes you feel less guilty, know that you *have* repaid the debt by allowing the giver to feel immense joy—a natural by-product of kindness. The giver feels immediately rewarded because he or she experiences what is known as a "helper's high." This takes place when the brain's endorphins are released and light up the pleasure centers that make you feel warm and fuzzy inside. If you are spiritual, you may find that the experience of doing good deeds touches your soul and makes you feel more alive. Both views yield excellent results. Whichever way you want to look at it, the results are positive and **payback guilt** is a needless emotion conjured up solely by you. We all share a home on planet Earth, and as a rule we should all be open to coming to each other's aid as needed. Feeling guilty because you believe you must repay someone's good deed is a defeatist attitude. Reciprocating in some small way to thank someone is noble, but once again, it's at your discretion as long as it is reasonable and there is no **payback guilt** attached to it.

Although you may never again cross paths with the person who came to your aid, all you need to do is thank him or her and be filled with gratitude. In the grand scheme of things, it was a special favor from one human being to another, and everyone should walk away from the experience feeling happy and empowered.

Here's a story about Sharon, a cancer survivor. When she found out about her illness, her daughter was only seven. Her husband had passed away two years earlier, and she was raising her daughter alone. While receiving treatment and convalescing, Sharon needed help from her parents who lived on the other side of the country. She decided to leave her home in Oregon and move to her parent's home in New York. Later, when she was in remission, she wanted to move back to Oregon, where she would have the support of a great group of friends, as well as the benefits of a lower cost of living. In addition, her daughter would reap the benefits of rekindling old friendships and be able to return to her former school. Sounds perfect, right? Wrong!

Sharon felt she *owed* her parents for caring for her during her illness. She believed she needed to be near them so she could reciprocate one day and help them when the time arose. As it turned out, Sharon's parents were perfectly healthy and even gave her their blessing to move away. However, Sharon felt so indebted to them that she refused to be reasonable about returning to Oregon. She sacrificed her future happiness, as well as her daughter's, because of **payback guilt.** The Guilt Monster had convinced her that it would be selfish to abandon her parents now that she was healthy and no longer needed them.

Sharon continued to live in an expensive city, in a depressing basement suite, trying to make ends meet, because guilt had clouded her judgment. The pros of moving back to Oregon outweighed the cons, but Sharon still allowed the Guilt Monster to color her desires in defeat.

A few years later, Sharon could no longer afford to live in New York and eventually made the decision to move back to Oregon where the cost of living was more reasonable. Her parents and friends were thrilled about her decision as they knew it would make her life less stressful. Eventually, Sharon realized she had been fabricating guilt all along because, after her move, her parents managed very well without her. She now understands that receiving help from others does not require her to carry the shame-wielding, scorekeeping, joy-busting Guilt Monster in her conscience.

Sometimes, people will do a *series* of favors for you, and you may feel overwhelmed by their generosity. Keep in mind that they wouldn't help you if they didn't want to. Life contains many cycles, and you may presently be in the *receiver cycle* of someone's good will. Guaranteed, one day the tables will turn, and you will be in the position to give, whether through material means, information, advice or offering compassion. Opportunities to give and receive from one another present themselves at will without much input from you, in a perfect time-space sequence. All that is required from the receiver of goodwill is to accept it and be grateful. When good deeds from others come sailing your way, send the Guilt Monster packing, because there is no price to pay.

37 PREGNANCY GUILT

When you feel guilty about providing adequately for your baby-to-be

IF YOU ARE AIMING TO be the poster mom of pregnant women by doing everything to have the perfect pregnancy, you may be setting yourself up for unnecessary disappointment. When you don't make it to your Lamaze classes because you have morning sickness, does the Guilt Monster look at you in disgust because you just threw up your baby's nutrients and missed an important prenatal class? Feelings of stress, self-loathing, and guilt heaped upon you, and your amniotic fluid wrapped bundle of joy, do not make for an environment conducive to healthy living. In order to deliver a bundle of joy, you must first *be* joyful yourself. Think about it. If you want to experience the best pregnancy, why not start by being happy, relaxed, and guilt-free, instead of allowing the Guilt Monster to rub your baby bump at its leisure? Babies in the womb are sensitive to feelings and sounds that surround them, so be conscious of putting yourself and everyone around you in a state of harmony.

When you become pregnant, it should be a time of celebration because the miracle of new life is in the making. Don't be tricked into thinking you are having a multiple birth as you carry not only your precious baby, but also the excess baggage of the judgmental Guilt Monster. **Pregnancy guilt** has the ability to tiptoe around well before conception as the mother-to-be scolds herself for each non-perfectly healthy morsel that touches her lips. Dear, sweet, mothers-to-be, do not live each day judging and lambasting yourself because you are not eating or drinking exactly what you think you *should* be consuming to achieve pregnancy perfection. It's wonderful to try to get your body in healthy condition before pregnancy; however, be reasonable about the journey.

The same mantra holds true *during* your pregnancy, when healthy choices are even more important. This includes not smoking, not drinking alcohol, and not taking certain prescription drugs. Eating organic foods, getting plenty of rest, keeping regular doctor appointments, and reading copious books in order to be as knowledgeable as possible are positive actions. The trick is not to give any credence to the Guilt Monster as it wags its finger at you because you enjoyed a sugar-infused cupcake. Get the drift?

You will, no doubt, indulge in foods that are banished from your pre-determined healthy diet that will momentarily derail your good intentions. This is normal, and has been taking place for eons. Fear not, my beautiful flower, it's permitted to enjoy chocolate-covered strawberries or a double Whopper with cheese here and there. Some days you will have outlandish cravings, such as pickles and ice cream with colorful sprinkles all neatly packed in an oversized sugar cone. This is most likely not on your current baby-bump menu, but while you indulge, enjoy it without the Guilt Monster trying to swipe it away at every lick. Remember, it's not just about *your* cravings; there is another living being inside you with cravings of its own. Trying to seek perfection in the pre-pregnancy and pregnancy phase is a laudable effort, but there is no such thing as perfection, so lean toward moderation and learn to go with the flow of the wants and needs of your body.

Also, what may be deemed "pregnancy perfect" to some is not necessarily perfect for YOU. Refrain from judging and blaming yourself every time you step away from predetermined cookie-cutter goals that are not working in your favor.

You should not feel the added weight of **pregnancy guilt** if you do not fulfill 100 percent of the "things you should be doing and things you should be eating while pregnant" list. Take the instruction of your doctor, listen to your body's needs, and relax and enjoy the beauty of pregnancy. In closing, embrace this special time, as well as every last drop of your strawberry milkshake, as you eject the criticizing Guilt Monster, singing its out-of-tune lullabies, clear out of your newly purchased pram.

38 PROMISES GUILT

When you feel guilty about unintentionally breaking a promise

PROMISES, PROMISES, PROMISES. LET ME start by saying that if you make a promise to someone and have every intention of not following through on it, shame on you! You deserve to have your conscience backhanded by the Guilt Monster in order to awaken you to your manipulative ways. By not intending to follow through on a promise, you not only disrespect the recipient, but you also disrespect your good name. You automatically set yourself up for unpleasant repercussions as others find out about your flawed character and learn to keep their distance. This chapter, however, is devoted to those who have good intentions to keep a promise but who, for reasons beyond their control, fail to deliver.

When life gets in the way—whether it is forgetfulness, busy schedules, or some other anomaly—and it interferes with fulfilling a promise, your heart begins to take on water and slowly sinks. You feel awful at the thought of disappointing someone, albeit unintentionally. When this happens, do not blame yourself and feel guilty about it. Instead, analyze what happened, and address the particulars of the broken promise with the person in question. This will alert the other person that you intended to keep your word but unforeseen circumstances intervened.

Promises guilt surrounded a father after he was unable to take his daughter, Emily, to the opening night of a new movie she was eager to see. Unfortunately, unforeseen circumstances occurred that interfered with his keeping the promise. When he broke the news to his daughter, her immense disappointment was unmistakable. He felt fried to a crisp from the megawatts of guilt sent from the Guilt Monster's power grid of blame.

Any number of things could have derailed this father's promise to his daughter, such as he lost the tickets, his meeting ran late, he fell ill, or there was a snowstorm and his car got stuck. His intent was noble but life got in the way. This dad unintentionally burst his little girl's bubble, which made her burst into tears. He was feeling the full-court press of the Guilt Monster's enormity pouncing on his culpable soul. His guilt was so overwhelming that he felt the need to take Emily on at least three big nights out to compensate for unintentionally messing up her special evening.

This emotionally ravaged father should not be subjecting himself to **promises guilt**. Naturally he felt horrible about disappointing his daughter, but all that was required of him was an explanation, an apology, acknowledgment of her disappointment, and his desire to make it up to her in the near future. This open communication would not only release pent-up guilt in the father, but would also positively affect his daughter by teaching her how to handle emotionally delicate circumstances in a caring and rational manner.

His daughter, although initially upset about missing her movie night, learned a lesson in coping with disappointment by realizing that life does not always turn out the way we want it to. She also learned that there is always a way to rectify unforeseen problems. This father respected his little girl's wishes by expeditiously re-booking their special night out. Soon, the duo sat happily together with their popcorn in hand while the Guilt Monster stood outside freezing because he was permanently banned.

39 RECYCLING GUILT

*When you feel guilty about
your recycling contribution*

THE OTHER DAY WHILE I was cleaning the house before work, I came across a few tin cans that my daughters had left by the sink instead of placing in the recycling bin. As well as not recycling the tin cans, they did not pull off the tabs that we later donate for the making of wheelchairs. Given that my time was limited, and because I was feeling frustrated that the recycling had not been tended to, I threw the cans in the regular garbage, tabs and all! The next thing I knew, a thirty-foot wave of guilt came rushing in on me with the Guilt Monster gleefully bodysurfing at the top of it. "How irresponsible! What if no one recycled? What then?" it exclaimed. Our planet's fragile environment is already drowning in pollution, and now I had added to its potential demise by not recycling a few pop cans. My conscience got coated with a layer of shame, a layer of blame and slimed with a final layer of **recycling guilt**.

Later that day I retrieved the tin cans, pulled off the tabs and put them both in the appropriate recycling containers.

This made me feel better. However, the occasional time you miss your recycling goals should not weigh so heavily on your mind that the Guilt Monster consumes you for lunch. It's not as if you are the president of a company that is illegally dumping pesticides into a city's drinking water supply and causing people to become ill or die. In such a case, a company's massive irresponsibility has caused bodily harm, and guilt would most definitely be warranted to awaken their conscience until apologies are delivered and solutions are implemented. Deliberately repeating such an offense of this caliber is quite different from not tearing off a tab from a tin can. This is why it is important to analyze *why* you feel **recycling guilt** in the first place and to discern if it is temporarily advantageous in order to enlighten you. If temporary guilt is used to obtain a positive result, learn all you can from the experience, then release the guilt to avoid wading through the tons of plastic debris the Guilt Monster throws your way. Commend yourself when you *do* recycle, all the while realizing that it is not always possible to recycle 100 per cent of the time.

Your neighbor has a compost bin in his backyard and has oodles of time to recycle every single thing in sight. Woo-hoo! However, if your time is limited and you are not able to be as gung-ho as your neighbor, simply do the best you can. I guarantee that the more conscious you become about recycling, the more you will find additional ways of participating and streamlining your efforts. For instance, I have perpetual giveaway boxes in my garage. As soon as I come across something I no longer want, it makes a beeline to one of my pre-designated boxes. Once the boxes are full, the items get delivered to its corresponding destination. Before I know it, someone will be enjoying a new wardrobe, appliances or books thanks to yours truly. I also give items to friends who donate clothing and electronics to countries in need. It takes only one phone call, and voilà! They swoop by to pick up the goods, and I've easily accomplished yet another recycling feat.

Taking reusable bags to the grocery store is another way to help save our planet, one plastic bag at a time. I keep reusable bags at the ready in my car and make it a habit to use them when shopping. However, there are times when I forget to take the bags with me or don't bring enough. When this occurs, the Guilt Monster sends me a video of all the plastic bags that ended up in the ocean destroying the wildlife, while I helplessly look on drenched in blame. Recycling guilt of this nature is unnecessary because my heart was in the right place, and I simply forgot.

Learning to gradually increase your recycling awareness and practices is a process, not a shame game. Do not allow the Guilt Monster to ruin your day because of small recycling oversights. It's no biggie if you forget the baggy; just learn to become more conscious in the future. At times, you may find it difficult to check off all the boxes on your recycling list; therefore, don't dump a truckload of **recycling guilt** on yourself as punishment if you are not able to do as much as you had hoped.

Another way to help the environment is to limit single-use plastics. Our oceans are so overwhelmed by plastic that fish are ingesting it, and subsequently we are eating it when we consume fish. Therefore, be conscious of every piece of plastic you use, and ask yourself each time whether its use is necessary. Do you really need a straw, which takes one hundred years to decompose? If you prefer a straw, that's fine, just don't feel guilty about it. Soon plastic straws will be banned anyway and will be replaced with biodegradable paper straws or companies choosing not to use straws at all. Instead of using a plastic cup with your plastic beverage bottle and plastic straw, try drinking right out of the bottle. You've saved one more plastic cup and straw from entering the landfill and oceans. If you want to take it a step further, the best solution is to carry your own reusable drink container at all times.

Plastics that make their way to landfills can take up to one thousand years to break down; that's a scary fact, especially for future generations. As these plastics decompose, they release harmful chemicals into the environment. Plastics will break down, but they never entirely decompose because bacteria cannot break through the links of their chemical bonds. Once plastics break down into microplastics, they remain in our food chain and are consumed by fish, shellfish, birds, and eventually humans. Microplastics, also known as microbeads, are found in certain soaps, polyesters, and facial scrubs. They are not ocean-friendly and are lethal to our water supply. To reduce your plastic footprint, visit the websites beatthemicrobead. org and myplasticfreelife.com to get started.

These are just a few ideas to help you gain knowledge about recycling and make informed choices going forward. Knowledge is the power that helps us propel positive change. I know you may feel guilty about your plastic waste contribution as you read this, just as I feel a twinge of residual guilt writing about it; however, instead of succumbing to **recycling guilt**, focus your energy on being pleased with your newfound awareness of helping our fragile planet heal. Effort equals results.

Rewashing and reusing your plastic cups and straws is also helpful. I also reuse my ziplock bags. I turn them inside out, give them a quick rinse, and then they are as good as new. Do I do this every time? No, I don't, but I do it most of the time; each step forward makes a positive difference. I also lean toward using reusable glass containers vs. buying more plastic. The practice of recycling requires a paradigm shift and is thankfully becoming the new normal. One simple recycling effort multiplied by millions of people will create huge improvements to our environment.

On one of my flights as a flight attendant, a younger woman and an older woman, not sitting together, made a beautifully conscientious recycling decision. During the bar service, when I offered each of them a plastic glass for their miniature plastic wine bottle, they refused the glass. I asked why they didn't want it, and both of them stated it was to help the environment by not adding another piece of plastic to our landfills. They proceeded to drink their wine directly from the bottle. I was moved by their choice and wondered why I hadn't thought of it myself. Instead of feeling **recycling guilt** about my past oversight, I thanked the women for the idea and have since shared it with many others. There are times, however, when I may prefer drinking out of a plastic glass, and that is my choice, but now I am privy to other alternatives, such as drinking from a bottle or bringing my own reusable container. Bottoms up!

As a sidenote, eating less meat also helps sustain the environment by limiting deforestation. Livestock also emit powerful methane gases. This is a huge contributor to global warming. (Just for the record, plastics also release methane gas.) All this information is food for thought and is only mentioned to add to your knowledge base and awareness.

In the meantime, I urge you to do your best to contribute to our planet's overall health by discovering additional ways to reuse and recycle products. You will also find you have less to recycle if you get in the habit of purchasing less, or buying items with less packaging. Find ways that work for you! If everyone makes an incremental effort to sustain the health of our planet, especially with approximately eight billion people participating, the results will be cumulative and impressive. Just do your share, and don't compare! Also, do not feel **recycling guilt** because you were not privy to certain recycling methods earlier that may have contributed to our planet's toxic state. That is in the past, and the past is no longer relevant. Start each day anew with your heightened awareness, and continue to forge ahead, finding new and improved ways to recycle and live green. In closing, do not allow the agitated Guilt Monster to slam-dunk you headfirst into the 7-Eleven recycling bin because you decided to use a plastic straw to enjoy your Slurpee.

40 RELATIONSHIP GUILT

When you feel guilty about how your relationship decisions affect others

RELATIONSHIPS COME IN ALL SHAPES and sizes, and each person you're in a relationship with has the ability to judge you if you do not meet their expectations. If you blame yourself for decisions that have adversely affected your relationships, the Guilt Monster will soon be giving you a private showing of its happy dance.

My carpenter, Jack, was undergoing the effects of **relationship guilt** after he decided to end his thirty-year marriage. Guilt silently slithered into his thoughts and released its venom upon the realization that his family and friends felt brokenhearted and angry because of his decision. Although Jack was well aware of the ramifications, he knew he had to do what was necessary to escape the grip of his lifeless, energy-draining marriage.

After Jack informed his children of his impending divorce and witnessed their disbelief and subsequent anger, the Guilt Monster lit a massive bonfire and gleefully threw Jack's wedding pictures onto the flames one by one. Jack knew that this was just the beginning of his **relationship guilt** that would be fueled by his family and friends. Let it be known that no one has the right to be the judge and jury of your relationship decisions, because *no one* is privy to all the inner workings of your relationships or how it adversely affects you.

The fact of the matter is that Jack could no longer live harmoniously with his wife, and it was taking a toll on him. When you grow apart from your significant other, and have tried without success to rekindle the flames of desire, the next step is to find a way to move forward. Usually this is in the form of moving out and being separated or getting a divorce. Eventually Jack's children would have to make a decision as well: either accept the new reality that their parents were divorcing or remain forever bitter about it. Either way, Jack should not feel a guilt-pinch about ending his marriage.

This was part one of Jack's **relationship guilt** story. The second part had to do with dating his friend's wife after his friend had died from a brain aneurysm. Jack had known his friend's widow, Candie, for a long time as they'd attended high school together. He was attracted to Candie back then, but never pursued her because she was beautiful and popular, and he thought she wouldn't be interested in him. When Jack was told of his friend's death, he immediately went over to pay his respects to Candie. That was when Jack realized he still had deep feelings for her.

As luck would have it, Jack was single now, and timing was on his side. He continued to console Candie as she healed, and eventually they began dating. They had finally found each other after all those years and were thrilled about how quickly their relationship blossomed. Although Jack's intent was noble toward Candie, he kept visualizing his dead friend wanting to pulverize him for taking advantage of his vulnerable wife during her grief process. Jack wondered if he was doing the right thing by seeing Candie and continued judging his every move while dodging the Guilt Monster's power punches of shame. Guilt ensued for a while, but after Jack discussed his **relationship guilt** with Candie, she assured him she was not being taken advantage of and that she wanted very much to be with him. The Guilt Monster, however, kept reprimanding Jack for alienating his family due to his divorce, as well as dating Candie so soon after her husband's death.

As an outsider looking in, I considered Jack's new union to be a blessing. He finally had found happiness again. I assured him that his dear dead friend wouldn't be upset with him, as he would not want his wife to be alone. And what better suitor than someone she knows and trusts? I congratulated him for being true to his feelings, and communicative and caring to all. This was the beginning of a positive trend in his life.

Jack left my house with a wide grin on his face and a hop in his step as he began to better understand his unsubstantiated feelings of **relationship guilt**. The Guilt Monster will no longer be burning the midnight oil, filling Jack's shiny bald head with blame, and will definitely not be on the guest list for his upcoming wedding or any other future celebrations. Mazel tov!

Another **relationship guilt** story involves a woman who became well known after her son murdered others and then took his own life. In an instant, this woman's life changed forever. She was entrenched in **relationship guilt** given her close association with the murderer, her son, wondering if she had erred someway in his upbringing. She immediately judged herself and wore the full brunt of blame for something she hadn't done. She felt responsible for her son's atrocious actions although she was nowhere near the smoking gun. She was desperate to find out why her son would commit such a heinous act. She continued to ask herself what she had done so wrong as a parent for him to turn out this way? She questioned her relationship decisions regarding her son time and time again. She felt culpable for the murders, as well as for having ruined the lives of the families left in the wake.

Through counselling and the tireless support of many, this troubled woman has managed to find some solace and meaning in her life. Day by day and step-by-step, she began to understand that her son's horrific actions were not a reflection of her parenting skills, and although the two of them were family, that is no reason to carry **relationship guilt** forever on her back. Her son planned and carried out his horrendous deed unbeknownst to her. Once this mom was able to take some time to process the event and heal from the shock, shame, blame, anger and sadness, she finally realized the murderous rampage was out of her control. She gradually stopped allowing soul-depleting guilt to ravage her psyche.

This mom now comprehends she must create boundaries to protect herself from the further onslaught of **relationship guilt**. Now that she's wiped away the film of guilt and can see clearly through a rational lens, she has made peace with herself. She decided to push forward, and make it her mission to help others suffering from similar scenarios by sharing her story through public speaking. Instead of living the rest of her days as a broken individual in solitude, she has learned to reinvent herself, and once again feel connected to others in a positive way. If relationships cause you upset and sorrow, make sure the Guilt Monster isn't part of your tomorrow.

41 RELIGION GUILT

When you feel guilty about not living up to your religion's expectations

ARE YOU NOT GOING TO church, synagogue, temple, or mosque as often as you feel you should? Are your relatives calling you an atheist because of your lack of religious commitment? Have you ever broken one or more of the Ten Commandments and considered yourself unworthy of peace of mind because you were less than a perfect religious ten? Are you not eating kosher, fasting, or praying when you are supposed to? Feeling guilty yet? If you answered yes to any of these questions, it's because you are judging yourself for falling short of your religion's strict expectations. Let it be known that no one is perfect regarding religions' strict guidelines, and therefore there is no need to feel ashamed and guilty of who you are.

Religion guilt manifests when you don't conform in every way to your religion's rules. Perhaps they don't make sense to you or you find some rules unnecessary. Whatever the reasons, you continue to fear the looming wrath of your Supreme Being's judgement and the possible hellfire to follow. I feel it is wise to ask yourself questions about your religion to see if it stimulates positive growth in your life. Get acquainted with what your religion stands for, and determine if you will benefit from its teachings. Beware of religions that utilize harsh judgement, control, and fear. Protect yourself from becoming a religious lemming by giving the teachings of your religion deep thought, versus doing what you are told. Wisdom and growth come from exercising your *own* thinking, not solely from following a belief system deemed by others to be best for you.

If you are basing your worthiness of receiving grace strictly on following the rules and regulations of your religion, you may be missing out on the other half of what religion is trying to deliver. Its main goal is to teach you how to love yourself and others by being compassionate, accepting and forgiving. If you are essentially a good person and trying your best, then falling short of a few religious guidelines is NOT a reason to enshroud yourself in guilt. Guidelines are put in place to *guide* and assist you, not persecute you.

While maneuvering around life's many temptations, it's normal to be led astray from time to time. If you feel you have erred in the eyes of your religion, it's in your best interests to give thought to your shortcomings, be gentle and forgiving of yourself, and learn from the misdeed instead of walking on hot coals with the malevolent Guilt Monster.

My mother feels pangs of **religion guilt** from time to time when she is unable to attend church every Sunday. She doesn't drive and has to rely on the kindness of someone to give her a ride. Moreover, she is oftentimes tired given her age and the great deal of caregiving she provides to her autistic son. I told her that in God's eyes, she is doing her best by caring for one of His creations; therefore, there is no need for her to feel guilty about missing an occasional Mass. As I see it, she *is* living the teachings of God by providing unconditionally for her son, and exemplifying the utmost patience, grace, love, and compassion while doing so. Religious dogma is solely there to guide us, not entrap us, berate us, or condemn us! Religion's main purpose should be to teach you to become the best human you can be, by offering friendship, compassion and forgiveness to others. Religion is not about receiving threatening and demeaning sermons from your wolf-in sheep's-clothing spiritual guide, the Guilt Monster.

Obviously, it's spiritually healthy if your conscience gives you a pinch, a nudge, or a slap when you have committed a *no-no* against someone. However, don't let a screwup prompt the hefty Guilt Monster to sit on your lap for every homily, making your thighs turn three shades of blue. Once you've realized your flaw, learn the lesson (and make amends if you are able) in order to avoid similar occurrences in the future. Sometimes there isn't a fault at all, as in the case of my mother not going to church. She is essentially a good person who has her heart in the right place; she simply felt the effects of **religion guilt** because she was somehow led to believe she is a lesser person if she misses a Mass.

When I was a young girl, I asked a priest if I could be an altar girl. He said it was impossible because it was against church rules. Only boys were allowed this position. It made no sense to me that I was not allowed to participate in the service because of my sex. I felt I was being punished for being a girl, and it made me feel inferior, unworthy, and guilty although I had done nothing wrong. Today, however, an altar girl is an accepted role in the Catholic Church. My purpose for telling this story is not to encourage you to disrespect the rules of your religion but to keep in mind that rules, ideals, and social norms evolve and change with the passing of time. The message of any religion should contain inclusivity, non-violence, kindness, compassion, and forgiveness, all of which fall under the umbrella of LOVE.

As a sidenote, I would like to add that no one should feel **religion guilt** about their sexual preference. I believe God created all and accepts all, and would not want anyone to feel inadequate or frowned upon. Being respectful of each other is what should take precedence, *not* judging those who do not fall within the confines of a religion's beliefs.

When a gay person takes his or her life because he or she feels like an outcast in the eyes of their religion, it is a tragedy. Once again, compassion, understanding, and love are the tools of God, not segregation, violence, shaming and guilt. Pope Francis reportedly told a gay man who was struggling with his homosexuality that God made him and loves him just the way he is. The pope also claimed that he loved the man and told him to learn to be happy with who he is. A bold statement for a pope after centuries of belief to the contrary, but this is additional proof that religious rules change with the passing of time through enlightenment. The only religious rules that will never change and that will always reign supreme are those that have to do with love and compassion. Make your best effort in life, and let your religious beliefs work for you in a positive way, not in a fearful, divided, and guilt-ridden way. No religion has the authority to judge you. If you are not intentionaly harming anyone emotionally or physically, including yourself, there is no need to feel **religion guilt** buffeting your gentle soul.

PS: If you can't make it to your place of worship, God's lines are open 24/7 worldwide, anytime and anywhere. Free chat time, through prayer, is always available to anyone, regardless of nationality, religion, skin color, sexual preference, financial status, etc. Do not let the Guilt Monster brainwash you into thinking you are unworthy of being in God's presence. You are worthy! And you are forever loved, no matter what!

42 SEX GUILT

When you feel guilty about not enforcing your sexual boundaries

EVER SLEPT WITH SOMEONE AND wished you hadn't, only to be left with deep-seated remorse? Obviously, you knew full well where your private parts were, but you wondered, *Where was my head?* **Sex guilt** has a propensity to manifest when you feel shame associated with having sex (or even thinking about it) for a variety of reasons. Feeling guilty about sex may stem from your strict upbringing, lack of boundaries, hurt feelings, or religious beliefs. Also, not being emotionally ready to have sex, insisting on the use of protection, or heeding the red flags of your intuition can also put you in the Guilt Monster's long shadow of remorse. Sometimes you are unaware of what your boundaries actually are before the sexual act takes place, only to to be cradled later in the arms of regret. Whatever the reason for your **sex guilt**, it awakens your conscience and forces you to focus on your sensitivity level, decision-making, religious beliefs and comfort zone.

Sex guilt can sometimes be instructive, as it's your conscience's way of helping protect you from feeling used, getting pregnant, or contracting a disease. It may be trying to awaken you to re-evaluate past sexual experiences and see if they fall within the confines of your self-protective boundaries. Review or re-write your sex boundaries as needed.

If you are on a date and you are not ready to share your body with that person, do not get talked into it because of your date's disappointment, and your subsequent guilt. If you believe in waiting for sex or the perfect suitor, that is solely your decision. However, always be communicative with your partner about your expectations and boundaries so he or she is aware of where they stand.

If the person you are seeing thinks that buying you a couple of dinners buys him or her a night in the sack, don't feel pressured by thinking you owe the person your body as a form of payback. To avoid such scenarios, it's better to go Dutch and pay for your own meal. This helps clarify any assumptions and prevents anyone from feeling taken advantage of.

When sex enters the picture, it is your body and dignity we are talking about. I've heard many stories of girls, women, boys, and men sharing their bodies when they were NOT comfortable doing so. A few of them got pregnant, some contracted a disease, and others felt used and violated. They later regretted not having been more forthright about their boundaries. Consequently, they felt **sex guilt**. Instead of needlessly subjecting yourself to swimming in a sea of guilt and regret about past decisions, utilize the information to become wiser, stronger, and more familiar with your newly etched line in the sand. Make necessary changes to your boundaries that will protect you emotionally and physically in future dating pursuits.

Your body is your temple. Sharing your body with someone should be a beautiful experience, not one that makes you feel hurt, ashamed, and guilty. Love and sex are not always compatible bedfellows; therefore, it can get complicated if one person is looking for long-standing love and the other is looking only for sex or a temporary relationship. Figuring out someone's motives can be challenging, as some people are master manipulators in fulfilling their agendas, particularly when it comes to their sexual desires. Make it your mission to find someone who is honest and respects your wishes in order to avoid future episodes of **sex guilt**. However, even when matters have been openly discussed, a situation may change at any time, so keep your eyes wide open and your boundaries close at hand.

It's always preferable to know what you are comfortable doing or not doing *before* you reach that critical point of having sex. Visualize, in advance, different scenarios and determine how you feel about them in the comfort of your own home. This will give you time to think about your options instead of submissively reacting to an onslaught of pressure instigated by fear and manipulation. Being hyper-conscious of your boundaries will make it easier to be direct and firm with someone, if necessary, so you don't get blindsided. When you engage in open and concise dialogue with your partner, the Guilt Monster will no longer have power over your decisions and will be immediately fired as your dating coach.

Engaging in sex is usually more satisfying when you know, love, and respect the other individual. Hence, one-night stands and sex where there is no history or long-standing cerebral connection with the other person may have you feeling like the Guilt Monster is a voyeur in your boudoir. Having said that, everyone has a different view of what they consider to be sexually fulfilling, so it is up to you to be honest with yourself, acknowledge how you feel at all times, and remain in your comfort zone.

Being selective about whom you sleep with should be job one! You deserve to be adored and treated with the utmost respect. During your dating adventures, you may have to kiss a few frogs and encounter some lonely periods as you wait for the arrival of a fulfilling relationship, but it is well worth it to get what you deserve! Instead of sitting around and moping, waiting for the arrival of Mr. or Ms. Right, use this time to get better acquainted with yourself and work on doing things that enhance your life. As well, figure out the qualities you seek in a partner so you'll be well aware of their presence when he or she is standing in front of you. As I tell my daughters, there's a bus every ten minutes, a limo once a month, and a private jet every few years. It pays to take your time and make the right choice. After all, committing to a long-standing relationship is one of the most important decisions you will make in your life.

Also, if you've been lucky enough to find the person of your dreams but you do not feel like having as much sex as he or she does, you shouldn't feel **sex guilt** about that either. Relationships and their inner workings are about give-and-take; therefore, communicate your wants, needs, and desires openly and honestly as often as needed. If you are not in the mood for sex, it's your right to have your decision respected, whether you are in a committed relationship or not. It's normal not to be in the mood all the time; however, your reasons should be openly discussed with your partner so he or she understands where you're coming from and doesn't take the temporary disinterest personally.

It's not always the easiest of tasks to discuss your sexual expectations with your date or partner, but the transparency is worth your peace of mind. Become increasingly familiar with your sexual comfort zone, and ban the meddling Guilt Monster once and for all from being a voyeur in your *chambre à coucher.*

43 SEXUAL ABUSE GUILT

When you feel guilty after being molested

VICTIMS OF SEXUAL ABUSE DEAL with immeasurable fear and guilt. The aftermath of sexual abuse includes not only the physical trauma but also the psychological after-effects. It is common to blame yourself or second-guess your actions leading up to the assault as you try to piece together what prompted the abuse to take place. Blaming yourself and later feeling shame and guilt is a temporary survival mechanism. You blame yourself because you feel you were responsible for provoking the abuse with something you said or did. You may think you made wrong decisions along the way, such as walking down a dark alley or staying too late at a party. As you try to wrap your head around how you may have prompted the abuse, let me shout from the rooftops, you are NOT the cause! Only one person deserves to feel guilty, and that is the perpetrator. Sexual abuse is a criminal offense and you are never to blame, it is not of your doing. If you were taken advantage of, manipulated, or forced in any way to have sexual relations of any type without your consent, the only guilty party is the perpetrator who committed the crime. Case closed!

When victims later reveal the abuse to their friends, colleagues, partners, or parents, sometimes their cries for help fall on deaf ears. The recipients of the devastating information are often shocked and in denial, and they do not want to deal with the truth of the matter or get involved. Other times, victims remain silent because they were threatened by the perpetrator, and told if they mentioned the abuse to anyone their families would pay the consequences. In these cases, the only life preserver available to hold onto is the Guilt Monster, as the victim continues to process the soul-wrenching ramifications of the atrocity in painful solitude.

After sexual abuse, coping mechanisms will surface that will help you deal with the aftermath of the cruelty. Initially, you may *deny* the abuse ever took place or question if the sexual activity should be given a label as severe as "abuse." You may *avoid* any discussions about it, *minimalize* its effects on you, and as stated earlier *try to rationalize* it and make up excuses as to why it happened. Your psychological wounds may also inflict post-traumatic stress disorder, loss of confidence, mood changes, sleep disorders, embarrassment, fear, and self-blame. These are normal reactions to trauma that register as *intense* on your inner "Richter scale." It is also normal for raw feelings of this magnitude not to disappear overnight; it will take time, and oftentimes the assistance of professionals to process your overtaxed emotions and start the healing process.

Triggers may continue to affect you off and on, but don't let them interfere with leading a normal life you so rightfully deserve. Although you are perpetually healing, keep in mind that this does not mean you are *broken*. You are both whole and worthy of the best that life has to offer. Do not allow your abuser, with a severely underdeveloped conscience, to become the gatekeeper of your happiness and power.

I strongly urge anyone who has been sexually abused to reach out to a crisis center or twenty-four-hour helpline. Enlisting the help of a professional or finding a support group is always advisable. If you are uncomfortable talking to someone face-to-face, there are counsellors that will talk to you over the phone, as well as online forums and excellent books that will aid in your healing. If you are spiritual, believe in the power of prayer, forgiveness, and fortitude that is yours for the taking if only you will ask. Also, instead of referring to yourself as a *victim*, which implies you are vulnerable, try to see yourself as a *survivor* who is resilient. Words are powerful and each word carries with it a vibration. Choose words that are positive that will grant you added power towards your recovery.

Many people have been known to rise above the damaging and hurtful experiences of sexual abuse. Examples are the renowned Louise Hay, an international healer and motivational speaker, and Joyce Meyer, the preacher who started Joyce Meyer Ministries. Eventually, they flipped their negative experiences of sexual abuse into a multitude of positive results by offering countless others healing through their own transparency and positive messaging. I highly recommend becoming acquainted with their books and audio and visual contributions.

Louise was a victim of incest as a child. Later in life, she was introduced to the philosophy of *The Science of Mind*, which helped her understand and overcome her past atrocity. She later created her own collection of inspiring books and CDs. She did not allow her perpetrator to win; instead *she* won by releasing her **sexual abuse guilt**, thus regaining her power! Another example is the famed Oprah Winfrey, who was molested by a relative. Although she experienced many trials, she overcame them and went on to become an emotional sounding board for the masses through her work as a television talk show host.

Healing is possible if you *believe* that each day holds the hope of a new beginning. Keep *hope* alive as it is extremely powerful and has a miraculous way of delivering you from the psychological wounds of your past. Be patient and kind to yourself every moment of every day. Be conscious of living in the newness of the present instead of reliving the misery of the past. If you go to a dark place, find the strength to be fearless; look your fear square in the eye, tell it what you feel, and then send it packing as you return to the light, where you so belong. Do not suffer alone in agony with the Guilt Monster as your only friend; the beast is toxic to your thoughts and has the potential to negatively affect your life. Instead, surround yourself with compassionate people and as much positivity as possible. Have faith in living happier tomorrows, and always believe in healing, forgiveness, renewal, self-love, and the BEST that life has to offer.

44 SEXUAL IDENTITY GUILT

*When you feel guilty about
your sexual orientation*

IS YOUR SEXUAL ORIENTATION NOT looked upon kindly by your parents, friends, or people you know or meet in general? Does your place of work or worship make you feel less than human? Well, I'd like to confirm that you *are* human, no matter what others deem to be right or proper. You are who you were born to be! We are all different and unique in one way or another; even identical twins have differences. That being the case, we should learn to accept each other's distinctness, instead of subdividing everyone into acceptable or unacceptable categories.

If you suffer emotionally because of your sexual identity, it may cause a backlash of guilt because you feel ashamed of who you are—ashamed that you do not fit into the stereotypical categories devised by society. Unfortunately, you will not always convince everyone to approve of your sexual orientation; however, you do hold the power to protect yourself from others' judgmental ways by not allowing them to brainwash you into thinking you are a suboptimal human being. If you are within striking range of their judgmental glares or taunts, it is in your best interests to distance yourself. Surround yourself instead with caring, like-minded people who accept you unconditionally.

As I've said before, if you're not hurting yourself or anyone else, there's absolutely nothing to feel guilty about. You must find the courage and strength within to stand resolute! We all have our unique paths of self-discovery; no two paths are exactly alike. Instead of embracing the abrasive Guilt Monster, embrace the true essence of who you are, and never discount your uniqueness and inner beauty.

A friend of mine was suffering **sexual identity guilt** and thought he was going to burn in hell due to his gay lifestyle. I soothed his nervousness about this admission by asking if he believed God would allow such a horrific ending to his beautiful life. He replied that, in his heart, he did not believe in such a cruel God. I told him, "As long as you are driving down life's roadways with love in your tank, how can that be wrong or frowned upon?"

Love is the key that opens life's many doors to immeasurable joy. If you feel the beauty of sharing unconditional love with another, how can that be deemed wrong? Pockets of society continue to frown upon the sexual preferences of others that deviate from whatever the current normal is. Normal is a perception of the mind, usually brought on by what the greater part of society or government dictates to be appropriate. However, in my mind's eye, other people's *normal* is their own business as long as they are respectful of themselves and others.

Do not allow the Guilt Monster to drag you through a soul-sucking swampland until you are covered in filth because of others' reactions towards your sexual orientation. Do not become dizzy with **sexual identity guilt** because your lifestyle does not please the wishes of others. If you continue to listen to the will of others and not love yourself for who you are, you will continue to flail on the spin cycle while others try to reform you by washing you clean. This is no way to live!

If the essence of who you are is being eroded by other people's negative opinions, stop the madness and protect yourself with boundaries and self-love. When you allow others to judge you, and when you *believe* their remarks, you also feel the need to punish yourself—yet you've committed no crime. Also, what gives others the right to judge you? They have no right to judge you unless you allow it! Do not *allow* someone's negative opinion of your sexual preference to create thoughts that bombard you with **sexual identity guilt.** You need to release these toxic thoughts at once and get back to loving every single cell of who you were born to be.

Start by creating boundaries that protect you from any unloving thoughts. Create a "boundary" binder and add to the list as necessary. When you fall into the trap of manufactured **sexual identity guilt,** bring out your binder for a quick review. Constantly be aware of what is triggering your guilt. Every time a negative thought rolls in, write it down, meditate on it, then dismiss the thought by asking it to leave. Replace it immediately with loving thought patterns because that is what you deserve—and nothing less! If you are unable to find the strength to do this yourself, be proactive and find outside means to assist you. Research different groups, online or otherwise, of people who will be understanding and helpful to your cause. Read books that focus on building inner fortitude and self-love. You will soon realize, through the testament of others, that you do not stand alone in your plight, and that habitual **sexual identity guilt** must be fought and defeated at every turn. There is no reason to feel ashamed of who you are. You are beautiful, you are special, and you deserve to be loved! Never surrender your power by believing in the insensitivity and ignorance of others. Granted, you will be disappointed, but that is no reason to allow others to make you feel guilty and trample your unique spirit.

To thine own self be true! This phrase says a lot and can be powerful if you believe it wholeheartedly. Give yourself time to meditate on its meaning. Be true to who it is that resides inside you. If certain people continue to find your sexual identity unacceptable, and if being in their presence becomes too stressful, limit your time together or continue on your path without them. Also, don't make it a habit of holding your breath, waiting for acceptance and compassion from others; you may have to wait a few lifetimes or more. Learning to love yourself unconditionally, without the approval of others, is one of the most beautiful gifts you can bestow upon yourself. Wrap your arms around every ounce of who you are, and tell yourself you are awesome, perfect, and loved. Everyone deserves to be joyful in the skin they're in.

The book *The Velvet Rage: Overcoming the Pain of Growing Up Gay in a Straight Man's World*, by Alan Downs, has brought comfort to many who struggle with their sexual identity. This is only one of a multitude of books, blogs, and websites available to help you find self-acceptance and inner peace. I always encourage reading as a way to comfort one's spirit. Finding solace in another's story creates inner strength and hope. When you read about the plight of others, you won't feel as alone in your plight—and you will come across a multitude of helpful advice. You have to live with yourself everyday; therefore, listen to your heart instead of the judgmental opinions of others who preach their righteousness devoid of understanding and compassion.

Be brave, be proud, be happy, and love yourself just the way you are. Giving up, giving in, and living with **sexual identity guilt** are not recommended options for a joyful existence. The only thing you should be giving up is your toxic association with the Guilt Monster spewing shame all over the beauty of your distinct God-given soul.

45 SUICIDE GUILT

When you feel guilty for not seeing the signs before someone took his or her life

SUICIDE IS A SAD AND delicate subject. One wonders why someone would be so horribly distraught as to do something so dreadful and final as taking his or her life. As it turns out, there are many reasons: depression, mental illness, drug addiction, guilt, and stress, to name a few. The realization that someone took their life leaves those left in its wake shaken to the core. Family, friends, and anyone associated with the victim are left breathing the bitter dust of the suicide's fallout. When you hear about someone's suicide, you are shocked, heartbroken, devastated, and angry, particularly if you knew the person well. Naturally, the closer your connection with someone, the more **suicide guilt** you are likely to experience.

After a suicide takes place, you instinctively try to figure out what pushed the person over the edge. You ask yourself why you didn't see it coming, why the person didn't reach out to you, or why you didn't take him or her more seriously. You wonder why you weren't more patient, understanding, and compassionate; why you didn't see through their nervous laughter or detect the sadness in their eyes. Alas, the Guilt Monster easily finds your open wound of culpability and infects you with a large dose of blame. Trying to find a logical solution to someone's suicide is impossible, because it is not rational. At the time the person took his or her life, they were not of sound mind. The person was having immense difficulty coping with life, emotions went into overdrive, the black hole of despair widened and every drop of their HOPE evaporated.

Unfortunately, most people see few significant signs, or none at all, before a suicide takes place. Some say they didn't think the periods of sadness, loneliness, or depression of a loved one or friend were "that bad." They didn't realize the full extent of the person's emotional suffering or that they were teetering on the edge and crying out for help. As well, those that are depressed can be masters at hiding their internal pain and sadness with a fake smile or laughter. This makes it virtually impossible to detect any underlying depression unless they reach out for help.

Processing your feelings after a suicide is difficult enough, never mind dealing with the constant jabbing rhetoric of the Guilt Monster repeating its claims that you could have done more, listened more, intervened, and ultimately saved a person's precious life. Unfortunately, suicide is not always avoidable no matter what you do to help or how much treatment the victim receives beforehand. You must realize and accept that you did your best for the person prior to his or her suicide in order to release **suicide guilt**. Initially it can be cathartic to come face-to-face with guilt for a short time, as it acts as a coping mechanism and helps you become aware of the gravity of pain you are in. But later, when you are better able to process the situation, you will see that **suicide guilt** is not the answer no matter what you did or didn't do. Unfortunately, people that commit suicide find the rigors of life too difficult to carry on fighting another day. It is equally unfortunate that it is not always possible to pinpoint the reason someone decides that suicide is the only answer available. In the end, there is no silver bullet, no all-encompassing fail-safe avoidance system. The best defense against suicide is to show compassion to everyone as much as possible, because no one knows what emotional turmoil others are truly experiencing.

When the healing process begins post-suicide, it is important to pick up the pieces of your life and stop racking your brain, trying to figure out what the hell went wrong, why you didn't see this train wreck coming, or why you didn't do more. Initially the grieving stage will be slow and painful as you examine your complex emotions. Reviewing the situation aids in releasing the buildup of energy stemming from shock, anger and sadness. However, in order to stop tormenting yourself with **suicide guilt** because you are unable to turn back the hands of time, it is best to accept the victim's decision and feel some relief knowing that he or she is finally at peace. Eventually, it is important to stop beating the drums of blame because you feel you did not go the distance to rescue a loved one.

Utilize a support system of family and friends to help

comfort you through the difficult days. Counselling, prayer, and spiritual guidance also offer emotional sustenance. If you are a private person, there are several online groups and forums that preserve your anonymity while offering emotional assistance. Take the time to talk to and pray for the victim, and wish them well in the spiritual world.

I heard a story of a father who lost his son to suicide. His son always found life challenging as nothing seemed to come easily to him. He had to struggle for every inch of happiness and self-worth. Approximately six months before his death, he'd asked his father if he could borrow money to buy a car. He had just started a new job that was located far from his home, and wanted the convenience of a car to get to and from work. Although the father had substantial savings, he would not give his son the money requested. He had helped his son financially in the past, but the son had a history of squandering money. This father wanted his son to learn to stand on his own two feet and become more financially responsible; therefore, he stuck to his decision and denied him any further financial assistance.

Also, months earlier, the son had reached out to his father emotionally and mentioned that his life had become too difficult and wasn't worth living. The father was in shock and denial at such a devastating remark. He retorted, "Don't be ridiculous. You'll be fine." I suppose his pragmatic reply was partially the result of his being overwhelmed from having heard such a heart-wrenching statement; after all, what parent wants to hear those horrific words from their child's lips? Perhaps the father thought his son was just sounding off in order to get sympathy and attention. Whatever the reason for his reply, this father was dealing with the situation as best as he was able at the time.

This parent would never dream of taking his own life, and perhaps he believed the same sentiments held true for his son. However, everyone's emotional state is different—some are more fragile or highly charged. It is difficult to discern, at the best of times, the depths of what another truly feels. Some people have a difficult time processing and sharing their deepest, darkest thoughts, and over time they feel boxed in, overwhelmed, and at a complete loss. When people are drowning emotionally and sending clues of wanting to end their lives, making statements such as "I wish I weren't here," it should ALWAYS be taken seriously and immediately addressed by a professional. Having said that, let me repeat, sometimes all the help in the world does not prevent someone from taking their life.

Unfortunately, a few months later, this father had to part with his money nonetheless—to pay for his son's funeral. In hindsight, he would have gladly given his son the money for a car, but at the time he felt he was doing the right thing. He now lives each day with a knot in his stomach as he feeds himself several servings a day of regret, blame, and **suicide guilt**. It is not easy for any of us to know what the perfect decision or action is at any given time. We can only do our best with the knowledge we have at present and hope it is correct. In the case of the father not giving his son the money, he thought he was teaching his son a lesson that would benefit him; and had acted out of love. Therefore, his guilt was unfounded.

If you've been affected by someone's suicide, find peace in knowing you did the best you could at the time with the tools you possessed. Please be patient and allow yourself the space and time for your emotional upheaval to even out. Healing will manifest more quickly once your blockage of guilt has been removed. If you continue to cling to the belief that you were somehow to blame for contributing to the suicide, self-forgiveness and prayer have the power to unlock the doors that withhold your healing. Although you will never forget the magnitude of someone's suicide, each day forward will lessen the pain felt in its aftermath. Be prepared for periods of both good and bad days to follow. Sometimes, when you are coping well after someone's suicide, something will trigger your emotions and you will temporarily regress. Allow your feelings to flow, knowing each day forward is another day to heal.

I highly recommend attending professional-led groups that deal with the aftermath of suicide. Talking about your feelings with others in similar situations aids immensely in the healing process and helps you feel less alienated. Writing in a journal also assists in unravelling your feelings and processing your emotions. The reasons people take their own lives are highly complex because the brain, nervous system, and soul are complex. There is never a single answer to WHY someone decides to take their life. That is why you must take the burden of guilt from your weary shoulders. It's NOT your fault. Although there is no elixir for deliverance from the anguish felt post suicide, I truly believe that your loved one is now in a peaceful place and would not want you to suffer on account of his or her decision. May you find daily strength in this time of trial, and may God, the warm light of hope, and the support and love of all those around you remove the Guilt Monster's shrapnel from your tender healing heart.

46 SURVIVOR'S GUILT

When you feel guilty about having been spared from harm while others were not

WHEN YOU ARE INVOLVED IN, or feel an association with a situation that has affected others in an unfortunate way, but left you unscathed, there's a good chance you will experience **survivor's guilt**. For example, it can be triggered if you lived in an area that got flooded where people lost their homes and lives, but you were unaffected, or if you survived a car accident yet the other driver (or passenger) did not. Soldiers, police officers, and firefighters who managed to avoid being harmed while on duty, while their brothers and sisters paid the ultimate price, also have the ability to feel the far-reaching tentacles of **survivor's guilt**. "Why was I so lucky to be in the right place at the right time while others paid with their lives?" or "Why did others succumb to their injuries but I did not?" are some of the questions people ask themselves when under the spell of **survivor's guilt**.

Survivor's guilt is a natural coping mechanism to help you process your shock and sadness after a catastrophic occurance. You immediately question all the *whys* of the incident in order to understand the event.

You may also wonder why you experience an *extreme* dose of **survivor's guilt** while others are not as affected by it, or do not experience it at all. Much of it depends on how your brain processes events. The more sensitive and emotional your nature, the more likely it is that **survivor's guilt** will have a considerable effect on you. Although being a sensitive person is a gift, it's also a double-edged sword. Not only are you processing and dealing with your own emotions but also you are capable of relating to the pain and suffering of others. This emotional overload can become both taxing and debilitating and it is important to protect your mental health by trying to remain as emotionally balanced as possible.

Initially, with the onset of **survivor's guilt**, it is best to *own* it. Allow every emotion the necessary time to be felt and acknowledged vs. immediately detaching yourself from it. It is a healthy way of dealing with shock, as it provides an opportunity for your overloaded emotions to be purged from your system. It is best to start by reviewing all the preliminary steps that led up to the event. Then, take a hard look at the final unfolding of the situation and what it left in its wake. You will begin to see that you have nothing to feel guilty about because the sequence of events that created the catastrophe was out of your control. If a situation is out of your control, then why feel the onslaught of guilt? Unfortunately, when an undesirable occurrence takes place, it can temporarily take the wind out of your sails as you try to wrap your arms around its enormity. You wish you could rewind the tape and stop the tragedy from taking place, but you can't. The damage has been done. The tape cannot be rewound. When you realize you are powerless to change the outcome, grief and sadness descend on you like a hurricane and wreak havoc on your state of mind. This whirlwind of emotions that spins in your thoughts is difficult enough to bear, so please do not compound your anguish by adding a truckload of **survivor's guilt** to the mix.

Although you will always remember the event that caused your **survivor's guilt**, you will eventually shift your thoughts from re-living the scenario and being guilt-laden, and focus more on thoughts relating to everyday life. This shift in focus will bring a return of normalcy and serenity.

If, over time, you continue to suffer from post-traumatic stress disorder (PTSD) or **survivor's guilt**, consult your doctor or a psychologist. It also helps to talk with others in a controlled group setting, because this allows you to witness firsthand how others, in the same boat as you, are finding ways to cope. Witnessing how others are managing their grief has a way of soothing your emotions, making you feel less isolated in your pain, and therefore instilling comfort and hope.

Events that occurred prior to 9/11 caused me to be infused with a huge amount of **survivor's guilt**. On September 4, 2001, seven days before 9/11, I was in New York and staying at the Helmsley Hotel. As I was walking through the lobby, I happened to see a peculiar group of men sitting at the bar. These men stood out and looked out of place, as if they didn't belong. I found this odd, as I would have thought everyone "fits" in New York.

The men were wearing pinstripe suits that looked like they'd been made in the 1970s due to their thick fabric and top stitching. Their hair was not crisp and neat, nor was it long and trendy. They were sitting at a large, round table strewn with pieces of white paper, minus any food or drinks. Four of the men had small frames and were hunched over the papers on the table, not displaying the posture of businessmen. The fifth man had a much larger frame and a larger than normal skull. His posture was bold and upright. He had what looked like a piece of wire, bent at a ninety-degree angle, jutting out of his left lapel. *Who on earth doesn't notice a huge piece of wire sticking out of their lapel?* I thought. My curiosity got the better of me, and I stopped short, just a few feet from these peculiar men. I was trying to listen to their conversation while looking the other way so as not to be obvious, but all I heard was mumbling. Then their voices came to an abrupt halt, and everyone at that table became deadly silent. I slowly turned my head to see why they had stopped talking, only to come face-to-face with the man with the huge skull. He looked at me with dark, dead eyes. The message I sensed he was conveying was unequivocal: If I didn't leave immediately, I'd regret it!

I froze for a nanosecond and then ran full sprint to the elevator, fearing for my life. My heart felt like it was pounding out of my chest. When the elevator doors opened on my floor, I looked both ways to make certain I hadn't been followed, then sprinted to my room and, once inside, immediately locked the door behind me. Pacing back and forth, trying to make sense out of what had just transpired on an otherwise normal sunny day in New York, I decided to call hotel security. I had my hand on the phone, ready to make the call to alert them about these scary men. However, after more thought, I decided not to place the call as I had nothing concrete to divulge other than the I'd received a bone-chilling stare that made me feel I was in danger.

Fast-forward four months later. I was at home watching a documentary about one of the terrorists of 9/11. The program mentioned that he had stayed at the Helmsley Hotel in New York one week prior to the horrific event. *Wait a minute,* I thought. *I was in New York one week prior to 9/11.* Then it dawned on me that the man with the large skull who had scared me was one of the 9/11 terrorists. The realization of my close proximity to this individual put me in a state of shock and made me feel nauseous. As I recalled that particular day in New York, I felt immeasurable guilt for not having alerted hotel security about the table of scary men, thinking that if I had, I could have saved thousands of lives. However, in reality, the hotel security wouldn't have taken any action, as there was no actual offense that occured.

I felt the ramifications of **survivor's guilt** two-fold; first, by knowing how lucky I was to have been spared from the terror of these evil men when standing only a few feet away from them, and second, by making the decision to NOT call hotel security. Although I was not at the World Trade Center that fateful day, I had regular layovers, without incident, in the very hotel that connected the Twin Towers. My having been spared from harm strictly on account of *timing* added to my **survivor's guilt**.

I have since done my homework, and now understand that feelings of **survivor's guilt** are manufactured. There is no reason to continue feeling guilty for your good fortune in the wake of someone else's tragedy. Carrying around the debilitating weight of the Guilt Monster has the potential to break your back as well as your spirit as you continue to question your good fortune. Unfortunately, most tragedies are unavoidable, and as much as you wish it were otherwise, they are completely out of your control. They remain a mystery of life; a fact you must try your best to accept.

Many soldiers who were fortunate enough to return home from war, while their comrades did not, also endure **survivor's guilt**. They feel guilty because their fallen comrades' lives have been cut short and their families are suffering from the loss of their loved ones, while they have been spared the grief and sadness of untimely death.

When you are a soldier, firefighter, police officer, or other service member, you are part of an extended family. If one of your "family" is hurt or killed, you are inclined to experience **survivor's guilt** because you feel you failed that person by not going the distance to move him or her out of harm's way. In reality, however, you did do your best at that given time, with the resources you had, therefore guilt is not necessary.

Be patient and gentle with yourself while grieving and healing. Keep the candle of faith alive, and I promise it will pull you through your darkest days and into brighter tomorrows. It takes a great deal of time to heal from shock, distress, sorrow, and heartbreak, all of which shake one's soul to the core and cause overwhelming anxiety and sadness. This is why it is so important to take the necessary time to work through your traumatic experience. Just try to not remain stuck in a dark tunnel of guilt and despair forever. Negativity only fuels more negativity. One way to push yourself out of the confines of **survivor's guilt** is by doing good deeds to those affected by the fallout of your tragic event. Volunteering, donating blood, or visiting families who have lost loved ones are all ways to help ease your emotional pain and lessen your manufactured guilt.

I know it's easier said than done to stitch together the jagged feelings you are experiencing in the wake of loss or trauma, but begin your healing by allowing yourself to dispel the blame. Luck is random, and fortunately you are one of the lucky ones. There is not always a rational order to how events unfold. This is a fact of life, and once accepted, you will feel relief. As fate would have it, you were given a second chance to live, so I urge you to take good care of yourself, make the most of life, and live large! Life is a precious gift; therefore, be thankful for every waking moment of your adventure and focus on the beauty that continues to grace all of your tomorrows. Through the power of positive thinking, you will possess the key to unshackle yourself from the ball and chain of blame, placed so maliciously upon you by the Guilt Monster.

47 WALK-YOUR-TALK GUILT

When you feel guilty for holding someone accountable

YOUR SON WAS IN THE habit of borrowing money from you with the full intent to pay it back. However, as time went on, it looked as if you would have to forgive yet another debt. Your poor baby still doesn't know how to *walk-his-talk* and be responsible enough to pay back his debt. In order to avoid any confrontation and looking like the bad guy, you say, "It's okay, precious; Mommy and Daddy will take care of that for you." Really? Why do you allow this unconscionable behavior to repeatedly take place? I'll tell you why: because the Guilt Monster has you in guilt lockdown and has thrown away the key! You feel guilty demanding that your son keep his promises due to a variety of reasons, such as: you are away a lot, you feel sorry for him, you want him to be happy, and/or you don't want to look like a selfish, unfeeling, moneygrubbing parent. Unfortunately, when you keep making excuses for, and coming to the rescue of, those who do not walk-their-talk, it sets the precedent that you don't mind if they choose not to uphold their end of the bargain. As well, you disrespect yourself by not expecting respect from others.

When a deal or promise is made, it's up to the person who made the promise to fulfill those obligations and *walk* his or her talk. You should never feel **walk-your-talk guilt** about addressing a matter of someone not holding up their end of the bargain. If your nephew said he would mow the lawn and he didn't, that's not *walking his talk*. If your friend says she'll see you at a certain time but always arrives late, that's not *walking her talk*. If your significant other said he or she would do something for you and then went MIA, that's … you got it!

If someone isn't walking his or her talk, ask why he or she was unable to follow through with their intent. If the individual finds that the question makes him or her uncomfortable, or embarrassed, do not feel guilty about it. You have every right to be taken seriously. Let me be clear: You are not doing anyone any favors by letting them off the hook, thinking they will figure out how to be responsible one day. Most likely the person will never figure it out unless you, or someone else, takes the unpopular stand of addressing the issue. This will enlighten the individual as to your expectations as well as make him or her conscious of not doing *it* again. If such behavior isn't stopped dead in its tracks, then the person eventually becomes dependent on everyone's forgiving nature, never becoming aware to the fact that he or she is in essence disrespectful. The unfavorable behavior will most likely continue until there's a day of reckoning, with someone who expects deals to be kept and *does* demand this person walk his or her talk. Irresponsible behavior is generally frowned upon by others and could lead to serious trouble down the road. The "don't worry about it" clause might exist with mom and dad, but it does not exist with landlords, credit card companies, or financial institutions.

If your secretary promised to pick up a time-sensitive document and didn't follow through because she decided to go shopping, don't feel **walk-your-talk guilt** when you address the issue. You have every right to do so. Unchecked irresponsible behavior has a way of snowballing. Therefore, it is up to you to reinforce your respect boundaries in both your personal and business life.

If you hide behind the Guilt Monster because you are worried you will be perceived as a mean, uptight individual, then you will continue to be treated like a doormat until you find the courage to make others accountable. If people can't walk-their-talk because they are unaware of how to *crawl* their talk, it is important to address it and stand firm with your expectations.

If certain people continue to not walk-their-talk, don't feel guilty refusing their requests, whether they ask for money, favors, or whatever! Fool me once, shame on you. Fool me twice, shame on me! Feeling guilty about addressing someone who does not walk-their-talk will give you nothing but aggravation, disappointment and disrespect as you perform in this D-list movie over and over again. The Guilt Monster plays the lead role and slimes you with its disrespect gun in every scene. Instead of letting this happen, take charge by putting your boundaries at the forefront. Find the lion in you and pounce on the meddling Guilt Monster as you courageously demand accountability when people do not walk-their-talk.

48 WORKOUT GUILT

When you feel guilty about not attaining your fitness goals

THE GUILT MONSTER STANDS BEFORE you in its workout attire, glaring at you in disgust and wondering why you are not fulfilling your workout goals as planned. You usually have valid reasons for not accomplishing your desired daily exercise regimen, but feel guilty about it nonetheless. I experienced **workout guilt** every time I sat for hours on end writing *Guilt Trip Detox*. A writer endures long periods of immobility. Because I wanted to finish the project in record time (which, by the way, never happened), I decided to forfeit my workouts and swallow the barbed guilt-pill instead.

One day, in the midst of writing, I got a phone call from a friend who said he'd just had a fabulous workout on his elliptical and felt great! I, on the other hand, had just finished seven gruelling days on the road as a flight attendant and, besides feeling exhausted, was catching up on my writing and a multitude of chores. My to-do list seemed longer than the Great Wall of China times two,

B

and for some reason *working out* rarely made it to my short list.

As each day comes to a close, although my intentions were noble, I missed my window of opportunity to exercise. The Guilt Monster shoots me a purple-eyed glare of disgust and once again throws my running shoes back into the dark recesses of my closet. I look squarely at my muffin top and blame myself for not making exercise a higher priority. With the onset of blame, guilt closely follows, creating a negative mindset regarding exercise and my health.

I usually feel intermittent flashes of guilt all day because I have not yet worked out, and then I have one big flash at night knowing my workout window has been locked and sealed. The Guilt Monster tucks me into bed along with my trophy of shame for not making exercise a more important part of my day.

The key, however, is not to blast yourself with **workout guilt**. This mentality will only set you back further given its negative spin on your psyche. Instead, be patient and positive with yourself and continue to make a concerted effort to get some exercise. You do not necessarily need to join a gym; just go for a walk. Try to envision yourself as a successful athlete to create a mindset of the importance of working out, and to keep feelings of low self-esteem at bay. When you think with positive vibes, it sets you up for success, instead of delivering energy-depleting anxiety and subsequent defeat.

When you are inundated by responsibilities such as having to cook dinner, take your car to the mechanic, pick up the kids, and perform a myriad of other tasks that require your immediate attention, don't harshly judge yourself for not being a superhero and finding the time to work out. When you berate yourself, your emotions will become taxed to the max and your heightened anxiety will exhaust you further, leaving you feeling depleted, thus sabotaging your intent to work out. Go with the flow of life's demands instead of putting yourself in a guilt-sealed pressure cooker if you miss a workout or three. Eventually you will find the time for a walk, a bike ride, a swim, stretching on your carpet or simply taking the stairs to your seventh-floor office.

If working out is a *necessity* because you have health problems and exercise has been prescribed by your doctor, try to be proactive and make it a priority. It's an investment that will pay huge dividends that the dishes awaiting in the sink won't. Squeeze in some exercise time by getting up a little earlier. Even if you're in a semi-induced coma, put on your sweats and go to it! Twenty minutes a day is a good start—*just get 'er done!* Do not answer the phone (people shouldn't be calling you at 6:00 a.m. anyway), and let others know that during your workout you are unavailable.

It's acceptable if you only have time for a short workout. Working up a small sweat is always better than no sweat at all. Just don't allow the Guilt Monster to pinch your love handles during your cooldown. If you still feel guilty about not having enough time to work out, walk everywhere as much as you can, take the stairs, and have a set of weights at the ready. Be in control of your workout by taking baby steps each day. And remember, it takes a month or two to develop new habits, so be patient while finding additional ways to add physical activity to your busy day. Be proactive about etching a workout slot into your calendar. Monday is a swim day, Tuesday and Wednesday are walk days, Thursday you get on your elliptical, and so on. Also, a lot of gyms, pools, golf clubs and yoga classes offer small packages for purchase instead of springing for expensive yearly memberships. This is a great way to diversify your exercise plan without breaking the bank.

If, however, you are sitting on your derriere in front of the boob tube or computer every night eating nachos and drinking beer, then yes, you ought to feel the Guilt Monster occasionally poke your spare tire. This is your body we are talking about—the vehicle that allows you to experience life! It's wise to keep it running optimally at all times. Just beware of judging yourself and feeling guilty because you didn't work out long enough, hard enough, or fast enough—and still don't look anywhere near the perfection of Barbie or Ken.

To sum it up, don't get out of whack because life has thrown you some curveballs and you don't have enough time to climb the Burj Khalifa for your daily exercise. That's okay. You are doing your best. If you continue to feel too swamped, maybe it's time to put something on the back burner so you are better able to take care of your precious health. All I ask is that you experience the lightness of working out, minus the Guilt Monster posing as your guru in his all-too-tight thong.

49 WORTHINESS GUILT

When you feel guilty accepting freebies because you don't feel you earned them

WHEN LIFE HANDS YOU SOMETHING for nothing, you may feel guilty accepting it wholeheartedly, or accepting it at all, because you didn't have to do anything to earn it. What on earth makes you think you are worthy of receiving something for nothing? At the risk of bursting your bubble, you deserve and are worthy of all the goodness that comes your way, whether you worked for it or not! Learn to embrace life's gifts as they arrive, and be thankful for the bounty that is bestowed upon you for no apparent reason.

Perhaps your apprehension to receive willingly stems from messaging you received as a child. Maybe you grew up believing that hard work was the only way to obtain life's many gifts and pleasures. Constantly examining whether you are worthy is utterly unnecessary. What is even more unnecessary is feeling **worthiness guilt**. This powerful negative thought puts the brakes on the universe delivering good fortune according to the law of attraction. Your feelings of unworthiness, that have been drilled into your subconscious for years, alerts the universe to stop the flow of *freebies* because you don't feel entitled. You have now created an opportunity for the Guilt Monster to take over your thoughts and play "you don't deserve it" mind games, and so begins the sad tale of **worthiness guilt**. This is a limiting and negative mind-set of your own choosing, no one else's. It is up to you to be conscious of your thoughts and choose ones that best serve you. Start by choosing to believe you DESERVE great things to come your way. Be open to it. Then, watch all the wonderful pleasantries that arrive when you least expect it. The key is to *believe* they will eventually arrive, but first, you must rid yourself of the self-imposed roadblocks of **worthiness guilt**. Accept all your blessings with grace, be thankful, and carry on. It's that simple!

The other day I gave my friend a bracelet I had purchased while in Beijing. I offered it to her because I noticed she was constantly admiring it. As it turned out, I liked it so much when I saw it that I had decided to buy two, thinking I could use the other one as a gift. When I offered the bracelet to her, these words came torpedoing out of her mouth: "Are you sure you want to give this to me? I feel so guilty." I told her that I wouldn't have offered it to her if I didn't want to and I would be thrilled if she accepted it. Witnessing her happiness filled me with great joy. My friend, however, was suffering from **worthiness guilt** as many of us do when good fortune floats in unannounced, and the cunning Guilt Monster swats our glass of plenty to the ground with one powerful swipe.

It is important to become increasingly conscious of feeling worthy, and welcoming with open arms the abundance life has to offer. It may come in the form of assistance from others, gifts, or helpful advice. You must believe you deserve the best and erase any negative messaging from the past. When it pops into your mind, send it packing! One way to become more aware of your thoughts is to keep a journal each time you feel guilty. Write down *why* you feel **worthiness guilt** and *what* may have prompted you to feel this way. Whether you find all the answers or not, this increased awareness in your thought patterns will assist you in becoming more in tune with the blockages in your thinking, which will in turn open you up to feeling worthy of all the goodness that falls on your lap. If you enjoy meditating, see yourself celebrating your good fortune over and over again, and feel the warmth of life's generosity tingle in your soul. Get comfortable with the buoyancy you feel from receiving good fortune with open arms, and DO NOT question it. Envision yourself accepting all the goodness that comes your way with a sunny smile and a gracious thank-you instead of allowing the Guilt Monster to photobomb your picture-perfect moment with its disgruntled mangy mug. Be mindful of expecting and allowing truckloads of goodness to come your way on the universe's wide-open highway of abundance.

In order to train your mind to feel worthy, believe you have already received that which you seek. Experience how it makes you feel to have what you want, then hold on to that feeling. Be thankful for your abundance in advance. This strategy helps train your psyche to expect many blessings to come your way. As you begin to believe you are worthy of the best, you will feel empowered, and that will attract even more of what you seek. Your new mind-set will crumble the Guilt Monster's barriers on your highway of plenty, allowing abundance to continue rolling your way uninterrupted.

50 UNCONDITIONAL LOVE GUILT

*When you feel guilty about
receiving someone's constant
and unquestioning love*

WHEN SOMEONE NEAR AND DEAR to you—usually a family member, friend, or partner—makes a continuous effort to have your back, forgive you, and love and accept every ounce of who you are including your imperfections, you often have a tendency to feel overwhelmed by this unquestioning devotion. **Unconditional love guilt** begins to florish when you've conjured up in that brain of yours that you don't deserve such tremendously deep affection.

When I would visit my elderly parents twice a week, I'd always offer my assistance by running their errands. I would also administer my father's biweekly injections to maintain healthy blood levels as Mom felt uncomfortable with this task. I always arrived at Mom and Dad's bearing gifts, usually home baking, groceries, or something unusual I had picked up in my travels as a flight attendant. Every time I visited, my mom would focus on my gift-bearing arms and immediately point her finger to the kitchen counter without acknowledgment. Without any eye contact, and in an agitated voice, she'd ask me to "just put it over there."

Eventually I confronted her and asked why she seemed so annoyed every time I brought her gifts. Her response was "I appreciate it, but I feel guilty. You're doing so much for us already, and now you're spending your money on us too. It's all too much!" I asked her if she enjoyed my company, along with my assistance, baking, and gifts. She said she loved everything, but she felt guilty that my frequent visits and gifts were *over the top*. "We don't want to burden you, you have so much on your plate already" she said. I made it clear to her that none of it was a burden as it was carried out with love in my heart and therefore felt effortless to me. Mom had ingested a high dose of **unconditional love guilt** because she felt uncomfortable with my steady diet of gifts and assistance. She was accustomed to being the nurturer of our family, and now *she* was the one being nurtured. For decades, my mother has always given, without question, to her parents, siblings, husband, children, and friends. Although my mother had no problem offering unconditional love *to* others, she felt uncomfortable and guilty embracing it *from* others.

My mom's **unconditional love guilt** in response to my acts of kindness was actually a double negative. Not only was she uncomfortable accepting my limitless caring, but her guilt-laden reaction ruined my joy as the giver. The Guilt Monster was double-ending it on this deal and laughing all the way to the bank of negativity to make a deposit. Later, after a lengthy talk, my mother began to understand why my unconditional love was not causing me strife, and therefore she had no reason to feel guilty. Let me be clear: Delivering unconditional love to someone is awesome, but it is equally important for the intended recipient to accept it with open arms in order for both people to feel its utmost joy. It is important to keep the scales of giving and receiving in balance and in harmony. My mom has since learned to embrace my love wholeheartedly, instead of tackling it to the ground with the Guilt Monster's massive linebacker frame.

I, too, had my own issues with **unconditional love guilt**. One day while on my way to the airport to go to work, my twin daughters joined me (as they were taking my car once they dropped me off) and my car started to shake and sputter, and then quit running altogether. We managed to get it started again and eventualy made it to the airport. My daughters, however, were in need of a car while I was away, and I was in a quandary about what to do about it with the limited time I had available before my flight. I didn't want to leave them with an undependable car in the middle of winter, so I decided to call my boyfriend for advice. While talking to him I burst into tears because I was so anxious and stressed out. He soothed me with his calm, steady voice and told me it was all going to work out. He always came to my rescue no matter what my situation dictated. He decided the best solution was to get my daughters a rental car at the airport until my car was repaired. He said he'd make the necessary arrangements and all I had to do was pick it up at the rental desk. Then he quickly said, "I love you," and hung up. Why did he hang up so abruptly, you ask? Because he knew I would feel guilty about accepting his gesture of unconditional love. *Why is he always so accepting and helpful of the many dips and turns in my life, and why does he continue to put up with it all?* Not only did he insist on making all the arrangements and paying for the rental, but most of all, he made me feel cared for and protected while expecting nothing in return. Later, when I asked why he continued to tolerate all my problems, he whispered in my ear, "Because I love you."

The Guilt Monster, however, tried to convince me that my car was *my* problem, and that I was taking advantage of my boyfriend's compassion toward me. I asked myself why I was so lucky to have such a wonderful man in my life and if I deserved him. Although I felt indebted to him, there is no debt to be paid where unconditional love is involved. Unconditional love has the power to see past one's troubles and imperfections and focus only on the positive.

Try to look at unconditional love as love without borders. It is displayed in sickness and in health, in the good times and in bad, with no questions asked and no balance sheet filled out. My boyfriend always had my best interests at heart simply because he cared deeply for me. It was a win-win situation. He felt wonderful coming to my aid, and I learned how to allow someone to love me for who I am, faults and all.

Stop overthinking other people's love for you. It is not your place to figure out *why* they do what they do for you. Whether you believe it or not (and I hope for your sake that you do believe it), you are a unique and vibrant soul, worthy of unconditional love at every turn. Allow the bounty of someone's unconditional love to envelop you without question! All you need do is be thankful and enjoy the ride.

Openly accept, appreciate, and give thanks for the free-flowing unconditional love that you have been granted, instead of gobbling up the manipulative rhetoric of the Guilt Monster, leaving you with a bad case of indigestion.

KNOW YOUR BOUNDARIES

IN ORDER TO AVOID BEING hurt or disappointed by yourself and others, it is wise to become best friends with your boundaries. Creating personal boundaries is similar to a country creating borders. Within those borders are a defined set of rules that protect it from harm; this time however, the country in question is YOU. Physical, emotional, mental, and spiritual boundaries that define who you are should be given deep thought. Creating personnal boundaries will protect you from harm and help you maintain a healthy relationship with yourself and others. When necessary, you may want to communicate some of your boundaries to others in order for them to better understand you. This will keep them in the loop of what you are thinking and feeling and allow them to better gauge how to approach you.

Boundaries create the framework of what you are comfortable doing, saying, and being. You will ask yourself questions such as "What are my expectations and comfort zone?" and "How do I expect to be treated?" This process will help you become better acquainted with yourself in order to create impactful boundaries. As well as *creating* boundaries, it is just as important to find the courage to *implement* them in order for them to be effective. As time passes, it may be necessary to re-etch your boundaries to better suit your needs as you evolve. Boundaries are a testament to the world of what you will and will not accept.

Are you comfortable saying a firm yes and a firm no to someone without hesitation or guilt? Are you aware of how much personal time and space you require to be fulfilled? Take as much time as you need to ask yourself questions regarding your *comfort zone* in order to create boundaries that will protect your peace of mind. Create a "boundary notebook" and start by writing a first draft. Modify and add to your list as you become more enlightened to what works best for you. Place the list on your bathroom mirror or fridge door, where it is convenient to review frequently. This constant reminder will help solidify your boundaries in your mind so they are always at the ready.

We are all works in progress, and our boundaries help us stay on the straight and narrow, protecting us from the demands and manipulation of others. Review moments in your day that made you feel cornered, uncomfortable, or regretful, and then, redefine your boundaries to better protect yourself. Become fearless expressing your expectations to others. Communicate them in a calm but firm manner and remain steadfast!

If someone becomes hurt, upset, angry or tries to make you feel guilty, do not allow your boundaries to become compromised or blurred because you feel pressured or feel sorry for them. Naturally, you may have to temporarily wave your boundaries if someone is in dire need, due to illness or unforeseen events, and requires your help. In these cases, as long as you are not in harm's way, a temporary boundary breach is acceptable. Use your wise counsel.

Everyone has different boundaries, and some have very few or none at all. Never compare your unique set of boundaries to others, because they are not YOU. Tailor your boundaries solely to suit your specific needs and comfort level. You will not be labeled a bad person or be less loved when they are utilized. If, however, someone judges you unfavorably because they are not in agreement with your boundaries, that is NOT your concern. Your only concern is to stand your ground and be true to yourself. If the person is obstinate and continues to disrespect your wishes, remain firm or remove yourself from his or her line of fire altogether. Listen first and foremost to your almighty boundaries so you don't feel the burn of regret later.

Boundary implementation should become one of your best friends. It will protect you more than any person will because no one understands YOUR needs better than YOU! Become accustomed to drawning your line in the sand by communicating to others what you find acceptable, or not.

Your boundaries represent who you are; therefore, you have every right to communicate them with clarity minus the Guilt Monster peering over your twenty- foot protective wall, looking down on you with contempt. You'll become increasingly empowered each time you find the courage to implement your boundaries. Some people, however, will never take them seriously, so it is up to you to build your wall of resistance high enough and strong enough that others can't obliterate it.

If you are one of those people who repeatedly blur your boundaries to avoid confrontation, hoping that things will get better on their own, I hate to inform you that this line of thought is not beneficial to your psyche's well-being. If you truly want to feel empowered, blurring boundaries is NOT an option. Initially, it can be difficult to stand up for yourself, especially when it is not in your nature to do so; however, in the end, it is necessary for the development of your emotional health, and happiness.

Get to know your boundaries inside and out, forward and backward, all the way up, and all the way down. Keep your boundaries' antennae high and in working order to keep from being sucked into the vortex of other people's agendas. If at first you don't succeed, push yourself to be stronger next time around. Eventually you will find the inner fortitude to reinforce your boundaries to the letter by voicing your feelings proudly and unequivocally. Wear your body armor of boundaries every day to avoid becoming the Guilt Monster's delicious prey.

FORGIVENESS

NOW THAT YOU HAVE BECOME familiar with the many faces of manufactured guilt that lure your buoyant emotions down a dark precipice of shame, blame, and punishment, you may add the final coat to your Guilt Trip Detox program: forgiveness. Forgiveness is the elixir to relieve your troubled soul from anger, bitterness and guilt you have retained from the past. You forgive, not because someone necessarily deserves it, but to free yourself from clinging onto debilitating emotions that inhibit inner peace. Forgiveness is a difficult life lesson, but once attained, it will grant you a sense of freedom second to none. When you have been emotionally wounded and wish to protect yourself, it is natural to want to seek retribution. It is counterintuitive to want to forgive. However, when you are constantly dealing with deep-seated feelings of resentment or guilt, it can become debilitating to your mental and emotional health, and the only thing that can set you free is the miracle cure of forgiveness.

Although segments of your past were far from perfect, and cannot be altered, your perception and emotions concerning them *can be*. Forgiveness is the only salve that will soothe the burn of emotional pain and grant the healing required to restore peace of mind. Will the scars of the past remain? Yes, they will remain, but through forgiveness, the emotions attached to those scars can be relieved in order to spare you from reliving the painful past. If you refuse to find forgiveness in your heart, you are doing yourself a disservice, because you are needlessly prolonging your suffering and carrying it into the future. You become repeatedly wrapped up in the wrongdoing, thus darkening the luminosity of your spirit. This mindset has a tendancy to create anxiety and depression and eventually a disconnectedness with others. Without forgiveness, your guilty past wins, over and over again. Replaying damaging memories, and attaching yourself to them in the same negative manner, keeps you stuck in a labyrinth of eternal misery. Having fun yet?

Start today and focus on a particular person or event you have been unable to forgive; the person could even be you. At first you will feel emotionally charged, and will find it a challenge to revisit your hurtful memory. If intense anger continues to reside in you, scream into a pillow, cry, or do whatever it takes to release some of that negative pent-up energy. Next, sit quietly and shut your eyes. Take several deep breaths in and out to relax yourself. After you feel relaxed, discover where you feel pain or tension in your body, then, with each breath out, feel the pain, tension, and anger leave your body. When you breathe in, see the white light of forgiveness wash over you, healing your emotions and granting you peace. See the black pain of negativity fade away in your mind's eye until it's no longer visible. Repeating this exercise (or others that are found on-line) will help peel away the layers of unrest in your soul. Eventually you will realize that you deserve the freedom of spirit that forgiveness has the power to grant instead of holding onto the torturous guilty thoughts of days gone by.

Sometimes, writing a letter about your internal suffering to the person you want to forgive can assist in purging your anger, resentment, and guilt. There is no need to mail it, this exercise is strictly for YOUR benefit. After you have expressed everything you want to say, save the last paragraph as a place to forgive the offender. Read the letter over and over, and forgive the person several times, as needed! Try to feel the release of tension in your heart.

Once you've read the letter enough and the negativity starts to subside, burn the letter in a ceremonial fire or rip it up and throw it away to help give a sense of finality to the matter.

Another helpful hint is to close your eyes and try to put a smile on your face while reviewing what or whom you want to forgive. This will reinforce the fact that their hurtful memory has no power over your emotions and joy. Your goal is to be able to smile all the way through the pain in order to show your thoughts who is in control. YOU are in control! When you do this, you will become more in charge of your emotions and feel both relieved and empowered. Feel the cleansing power of forgiveness wash over you like a warm, gentle breeze while you repeatedly say goodbye to outdated thoughts and feelings that dilute your hope and happiness. As mentioned earlier, the memory will prevail, but you have the ability to alter the emotions attached to it by looking at them one last time and saying your goodbyes. It is also advisable to pray, meditate (many great meditations on-line), get counselling, read self-help books, or release your feelings with a good friend.

Forgiveness puts you in the driver's seat of your emotions, where you rightfully belong. The whole point of forgiveness is not to discount the pain you experienced, allow your perpetrator a free pass, or obliterate the event from your memory, but to allow you to continue living with a light and free spirit versus a heavy spirit filled with spite, hate, remorse and guilt. Which will you choose?

It is also helpful to become aware of emotional triggers in order to spare yourself from reliving painful memories while on the road to forgiveness. When a negative feeling or memory comes back to haunt you, tell it it is no longer welcome and focus on immediately changing your line of thought. Each step forward loosens the negative particles from your heart and brings you closer to peace. When you plant the seed of forgiveness, it will eventually blossom and push out the weeds of anger, disappointment and guilt that were the gatekeepers of your joy.

Become familiar with the cleansing power of forgiveness while you repeatedly say goodbye to outdated thoughts and feelings that dilute your hope and happiness. Every time you do this you are on the road to being granted many miracles, one of which is the release of emotional burdens that perpetually weigh you down. Forgiveness will release the slow burn of emotional pain. You will see the world through happier, gentler eyes and will be able to retire your boxing gloves, as there is no longer a need to defend yourself. Forgiveness is a choice, so choose wisely and make it happen! Do not allow your ego to circumvent your healing. Ego has the potential to become a major stumbling block on your road to forgiveness. Thankfully the miracle of forgiveness is always on standby and ready when you are, just say the word!

As a side note; if the person you are trying to forgive is still a part of your life, it doesn't mean you must hang out with him or her and do lunch. Just be aware of the person's tactics so you don't get tangled up in their misery again, and keep your time with him or her to a minimum, if at all. The key to forgiveness is to condition yourself to stop carrying the person in question around rent free in your mind. Be selfish and do yourself a favor by learning to forgive and move on.

I would like to share a story about a rather sad-looking clerk I befriended at a health store. She started chatting about how different parts of our bodies hold on to emotional pain. As an example, she divulged that when she was a child, her father had abused her physically and emotionally, and she carries this pain in her liver. She said she withheld much anger toward him and somehow blamed herself for his reprehensible actions and felt guilty. I told her that his actions were in no way her fault and that she was experiencing the effects of manufactured guilt. I also mentioned that if she is able to forgive her father (even a little) it would alleviate her burden of anger and guilt, and she would feel more inner peace. The forgiveness is NOT for the benefit of her father, it is for HER benefit! Not being able to forgive, even a little, can easily take a toll on your health because the mind and body are interconnected, and when one is out of sync, so is the other. We talked for a while longer, and I recommended the titles of a few books that I felt would aid in her journey, one of which was *A Return to Love* by Marianne Williamson. Before we parted ways, the woman found her smile again as she realized her future held the hope of newfound peace and renewal.

By choosing to forgive all of life's imperfections, you are now in the coveted position to reclaim your ease of spirit! Allow forgiveness to heal your heart and free your mind, melting away the dis-ease of the Guilt Monster one thought at a time.

CONCLUSION

*It is my hope that the contents
of Guilt Trip Detox have helped
you heal from the ramifications of
manufactured guilt. You now possess
the tools to acknowledge it, grow
from it, purge it from your system,
and avoid its wrath in the future.*

THE DEVIOUS GUILT MONSTER HAS been exposed under the bright white light of your examination room, identifying fifty types of guilt. Although there are many more, you should have enough information to be able to recover from all other forms of *guilt-itis*.

While you send the Guilt Monster blasting into the unknown, have a blast yourself as you celebrate removing the binding chains of guilt from your weary soul. None of us is perfect, so, at the very most, guilt should act only as a temporary nudge in order to lead us to learn, not as a means to perpetually torment. Step-by-step and day by day, live guilt-free and retain a tranquil and joyful mind.

May you lift your spirit by living guilt-free, and may the wisdom that you have acquired from *Guilt Trip Detox* multiply as you share your knowledge and positive results with others. Love yourself, love others, love the planet, and listen daily to your internal messaging. You are unique! You are whole! You are perfect! (Albeit in an imperfect world.) Quit towing around the extra weight of the debilitating Guilt Monster as you continue your road trip through life. Unhitch the burly beast from your thoughts, and feel the serenity of living your life to the fullest and guilt-free. May your continued travels be safe, joyful, and full of wonder! Love to all!

If you have any comments or stories you care to share, feel free to contact the GUILT GURU at:
www.guilttripdetox.com

Printed in the United States
By Bookmasters